# REVISE EDEXCEL GCSE
# French

# REVISION GUIDE

Series Consultant: Harry Smith          Authors: Rosi McNab and Harriette Lanzer

## THE REVISE EDEXCEL SERIES
### Available in print or online

Online editions for all titles in the Revise Edexcel series are available Autumn 2012.

Presented on our ActiveLearn platform, you can view the full book and customise it by adding notes, comments and weblinks.

### Print editions

| | |
|---|---|
| French Revision Guide | 9781446903476 |
| French Revision Workbook | 9781446903346 |

### Online editions

| | |
|---|---|
| French Revision Guide | 9781446903384 |
| French Revision Workbook | 9781446903377 |

This Revision Guide is designed to complement your classroom and home learning, and to help prepare you for the exam. It does not include all the content and skills needed for the complete course. It is designed to work in combination with Edexcel's main GCSE French 2009 Series.

**To find out more visit:**
www.pearsonschools.co.uk/edexcelgcseMFLrevision

ALWAYS LEARNING          PEARSON

# Contents

1-to-1 page match with the French Revision Workbook ISBN 9781446903346

## Audio files

Audio files for the listening exercises in this book can be found at: www.pearsonschools.co.uk/mflrevisionaudio

## A small bit of small print

Edexcel publishes Sample Assessment Material and the Specification on its website. This is the official content and this book should be used in conjunction with it. The questions in *Now try this* have been written to help you practise every topic in the book. Remember: the real exam questions may not look like this.

## Target grades

Target grades are quoted in this book for some of the questions. Students targeting this grade should be aiming to get most of the marks available. Students targeting a higher grade should be aiming to get all of the marks available.

# Birthdays

You need to recognise dates in reading and listening questions, so learn months and numbers.

## Les anniversaires

| | |
|---|---|
| J'ai 16 ans. | I am 16 years old. |
| le premier mars | 1st March |
| le vingt-et-un avril | 21st April |
| le trente-et-un juillet | 31st July |
| le douze mai | 12th May |
| Quelle est la date de ton anniversaire? | When is your birthday? |
| Mon anniversaire est (le trois avril). | My birthday is (3rd April). |

janvier
février
mars
avril
mai
juin
juillet
août
septembre
octobre
novembre
décembre

## Alphabet

**LISTENING 1**

Comment ça s'écrit?
How do you spell that?

### L'alphabet

| A AH | N EN | Accents |
|---|---|---|
| B BAY | O OH | é accent aigu |
| C SAY | P PAY | è accent |
| D DAY | Q COO | grave |
| E EUH | R ERR | ê circonflexe |
| F EFF | S ESS | ç cédille |
| G DJAY | T TAY | – trait d'union |
| H ASH | U OO | |
| I EE | V VAY | |
| J DJEE | W DOOBL-VAY | |
| K KAH | X EEX | |
| L ELL | Y EE-GREK | |
| M EM | Z ZED | |

Watch out for the letters in red! Check your alphabet by spelling the English address FAIRVIEW GRANGE.

## Worked example

**LISTENING 2**  **target E**

Listen and complete the ID form for this exchange student.

Name: Justine

Age: 15

Birthday: 2 September

– Je me présente. Je m'appelle Justine.
Ça s'écrit J U S T I N E.
J'ai quinze ans. Mon anniversaire est le deux septembre.

## EXAM ALERT!

Students often spell names and places incorrectly in their listening exam. The speaker tells you how to spell Justine's name, so you have to spell it correctly. Listen carefully, and make sure you know your alphabet.

Students have struggled with exam questions similar to this – **be prepared!**  ResultsPlus

Don't muddle numbers such as **deux** (2) with **douze** (12).

## Now try this

**LISTENING 3**  **target E**

Listen to four more exchange students introducing themselves and note down their details.

• Name   • Age   • Birthday

Check that you could give these details about yourself, if asked.

# Physical description

This page will help you describe yourself and others. Remember to make adjectives agree!

## Mon look

| | |
|---|---|
| Je suis grand(e) / petit(e). | I am tall / small. |
| Il / Elle est de taille moyenne. | He / She is of average height. |
| Je suis mince / gros(se). | I am thin / fat. |
| J'ai les cheveux courts / longs / mi-longs. | I've got short / long / medium-length hair. |
| bouclés / frisés | curly |
| raides | straight |
| roux / noirs / blonds | red / black / blonde |
| châtains / marron | chestnut / brown |
| J'ai les yeux bleus / gris. | I've got blue / grey eyes. |
| barbe (f) | beard |
| lunettes (fpl) | glasses |
| nez (m) | nose |
| Il / Elle est beau / belle. | He / She is good-looking. |
| Je le / la trouve laid(e). | I think he / she is ugly. |
| Elle est assez jolie. | She is quite pretty. |

### Irregular adjectives: vieux and beau

Page 81

| | singular | | plural | |
|---|---|---|---|---|
| | masc | fem | masc | fem |
| old | vieux | vieille | vieux | vieilles |
| beautiful | beau | belle | beaux | belles |

vieil and bel (for nouns starting with a vowel or silent h).

Mon père est assez vieux.

Ma soeur est très belle.

---

## Worked example

Write a description of yourself.

Je suis assez grand mais un peu trop gros. J'ai les yeux bleu-gris et les cheveux mi-longs et blonds. Ma sœur est jolie mais elle est trop mince.

This answer uses modifiers like **assez** and **trop**. It makes the answer easier to read and more interesting.

**AIMING HIGHER**

Quand j'étais petite, j'avais les cheveux longs, blonds et frisés, mais à l'âge de treize ans j'ai découvert un nouveau look! Je suis allée chez le coiffeur et je lui ai demandé de me teindre les cheveux en vert. Quand ils sont rentrés à la maison, mes parents étaient vraiment fâchés. Maintenant j'ai un piercing discret que personne ne peut voir!

- This answer uses three different tenses – imperfect, perfect and present. It avoids repeating the noun and helps the text flow.
- Notice the use of the pronoun **lui**, too.

se teindre les cheveux = to dye one's hair

### Golden rules

1 VARY YOUR TENSES – your answers will be more interesting if you write about events which happened in the past.

2 MAKE IT STAND OUT – an unusual twist might make your work stand out from the crowd, e.g. j'ai un piercing discret que personne ne peut voir (I've got a piercing which nobody can see!)

---

## Now try this

Write a description of yourself or a friend, in about 100 words.

Make sure you use:
- modifiers (assez, trop, très)
- correct adjective agreements.

# Character description

You may need to be able to describe somebody's personality. If you are describing real people, remember to be *sympa* (nice) and *sensible* (sensitive) to their feelings.

## La personnalité

| Il / Elle a l'air ... | He / She looks ... |
| --- | --- |
| agaçant(e) | annoying |
| (dés)agréable | (un)pleasant |
| amical(e) | friendly |
| amusant(e), marrant(e) | funny |
| animé(e) | lively |
| bavard(e) | chatty |
| bête | silly |
| de bonne / mauvaise humeur | in a good / bad mood |
| drôle | funny / witty |
| en colère | angry |
| désordonné(e) | untidy |
| gentil(le) | nice / kind |
| méchant(e), vilain(e) | mean, nasty |
| paresseux / paresseuse | lazy |
| (im)poli(e) | (im)polite |
| sage | well-behaved |
| timide | shy |
| triste | sad |

### Object pronouns
Page 86

Using PRONOUNS can help you avoid repeating the noun.

| me | me | us | nous |
| --- | --- | --- | --- |
| you | te | you | vous |
| him / it | le | them | les |
| her / it | la | | |

Vowel / Silent h + me, te, le, la = m', t', l'

Le sport ne l'intéresse pas.
Sport doesn't interest him.

Russell Howard est amusant mais il est parfois méchant.

---

## Worked example
LISTENING 4   target D

Jamel is talking about his best friend Joachim.
Put a cross by the word that describes Joachim.

funny ☒    noisy ☐    lazy ☐

– Joachim est très amusant mais il n'aime pas sortir en groupe, il n'aime pas le bruit.

## EXAM ALERT!

As well as requiring you to listen to a continuous extract, this question asks you to recognise negatives as well. You also need to distinguish clearly between **je** and **il / elle**.

Students have struggled with exam questions similar to this – **be prepared!**   Result Plus

The adjective **amusant** (funny) is mentioned here, but the word **bruit** (noise) appears with a negative form: il n'aime pas le bruit. You need to concentrate on the **meaning**, not just the individual words you hear.

---

## Now try this
LISTENING 5   target D

Listen to the rest of the description and put a cross by the four correct letters which describe Joachim.

| | | | | |
| --- | --- | --- | --- | --- |
| **A** keen on sport | ☐ | **E** generous | ☐ | |
| **B** messy | ☐ | **F** noisy | ☐ | |
| **C** sometimes bad-tempered | ☐ | **G** understanding | ☐ | |
| **D** lazy | ☐ | **H** impatient | ☐ | |

Listen carefully for who really is de mauvaise humeur: Joachim (il) or Jamel (je).

# Where you live

If you are writing as a girl, you need to make sure you have the correct ending to all adjectives which relate to you – don't forget about them halfway through your answer!

## Mon pays

All these countries are feminine.

| Country | Nationality (adj) |
|---|---|
| Belgique | belge |
| Angleterre | anglais(e) |
| France | français(e) |
| Allemagne | allemand(e) |
| Grande-Bretagne | britannique |
| Grèce | grec / grecque |
| Irlande | irlandais(e) |
| Italie | italien(ne) |
| Écosse | écossais(e) |
| Espagne | espagnol(e) |
| Suisse | suisse |

## 'in' + country

To say 'in' with names of countries, use the following:

| masc | fem | plural |
|---|---|---|
| au | en | aux |

J'habite en Angleterre.   I live in England.

J'ai passé les vacances au pays de Galles.
I spent the holiday in Wales.

Je voudrais étudier aux États-Unis.
I would like to study in the US.

Note that these countries are masculine:

Pays-Bas (mpl)   Netherlands

Royaume-Uni (m)   United Kingdom

États-Unis (mpl)   United States

pays de Galles (m)   Wales

## Worked example

Write about where you live.

Je suis écossaise. J'habite à Grantham en Angleterre depuis cinq ans mais je suis née à Édimbourg, en Écosse.

**AIMING HIGHER** Je préfère habiter en Angleterre plutôt qu'en Écosse parce que j'aime l'ambiance ici. L'endroit où j'habite est animé et près des commerces, mais mes amis qui habitent encore en Écosse me manquent beaucoup. Alors cette année je vais leur rendre visite et ça va être chouette, j'en suis sûre.

This student has included the correct agreements on écossaise (Scottish) and née (born), as she is a girl.

This student has raised her level by comparing the two countries, using words such as où (the place where I live) and looking ahead with the near future je vais leur rendre visite (I am going to visit them).

## Developing your answer

Always look for opportunities to add more information to your written work. You could:

- say how long you have lived somewhere
- say where you were born (Je suis né(e) à / en ...)
- give your opinion.

## Now try this

Answer these questions in French. Write about 100 words.

- Vous êtes de quelle nationalité?
- Où êtes-vous né(e)?
- Où habitez-vous maintenant? Vous trouvez l'endroit comment?
- Où voudriez-vous habiter à l'âge de 21 ans? Pourquoi?

Check your written work for:
- correct endings on adjectives and past participles
- accents on words which need them.

# Family

This page will prepare you to say lots about your brothers and sisters!

## La famille

| | |
|---|---|
| demi-frère (m) | half-brother |
| demi-sœur (f) | half-sister |
| beau-frère (m) | stepbrother |
| belle-sœur (f) | stepsister |
| jumeaux (mpl) / jumelles (fpl) | twins |
| Je suis l'aîné(e). | I am the oldest. |
| Je suis enfant unique. | I am an only child. |
| J'adore ma sœur cadette. | I love my younger sister. |
| Ma grande sœur est autoritaire / égoïste. | My big sister is bossy / selfish. |
| Mon petit frère est toujours (im)poli. | My little brother is always (im)polite. |
| Mon frère aîné est insupportable. | My oldest brother is unbearable. |
| Il m'embête / m'énerve. | He annoys me. |
| Ma belle-sœur est agaçante. | My stepsister is annoying. |

## Using on

- The pronoun on is used a lot in French. It can mean 'we', 'you' or 'one'.
- It takes the same part of the verb as il / elle.

On s'amuse bien ensemble.
We have fun together.
On s'entend bien.
We get on well.
On peut tout se dire.
We can say anything to each other.
On se dispute beaucoup.
We quarrel a lot.

## Worked example

Write about your brothers and sisters.

J'ai deux sœurs qui s'appellent Alice et Wendy. Elles se disputent sans cesse. Je m'entends bien avec Alice parce qu'on s'amuse bien ensemble et on aime la même musique. Cependant, je ne m'entends pas bien avec Wendy parce qu'elle est trop égoïste, elle n'aide pas à la maison et on se dispute toujours.

This makes good use of the relative pronoun qui (who), a variety of verb forms je, elles, elle, on and opinions + reasons. BUT there is no variety of tenses, which means this student is unlikely to get a very high grade.

This student uses three tenses: the imperfect to say what his relationship with his brother used to be like and the present to compare that with how things are now. He also uses the future to talk about weekend plans.

**AIMING HIGHER**
J'ai un frère et une sœur. Quand j'étais plus jeune, je ne m'entendais pas bien avec mon petit frère parce qu'il était un véritable casse-pieds et je devais m'occuper de lui, mais maintenant on joue au foot et aux jeux vidéo ensemble et on s'entend mieux. Ce weekend je vais lui apprendre à nager.

## Aiming higher

If you are aiming for a top grade, you need to do the following.

1. Include more complex sentences.
2. Justify your opinions.
3. Use elements such as comparatives (mieux – better) and indirect pronouns (lui – him).

## Now try this

Answer these questions about your brothers and sisters. Write about 100 words.

- Vous avez des frères et sœurs? Pouvez-vous les décrire?
- Vous vous entendez bien avec vos frères / sœurs? Pourquoi (pas)?
- Comment serait votre frère / sœur idéal(e)?

# Describing my family

This page will help you talk about your family, even if it's a complicated one.

## Ma famille

mère — mother
femme — wife
grand-mère — grandmother

père — father
mari — husband

grands-parents — grandparents

grand-père — grandfather

fils — son
fille — daughter

| | |
|---|---|
| cousin (m) / cousine (f) | cousin |
| maman (f) | mum |
| mamie / mémé (f) | nana, gran |
| oncle (m) | uncle |
| papa (m) | dad |
| papy / pépé (m) | granddad |
| petit(e)-enfant (m/f) | grandchild |
| tante (f) | aunt |

## Using ne … plus

Il n'habite plus chez nous.
He doesn't live with us any more.
Il ne reste plus rien.
There isn't anything left.

| Il / Elle est … | He / She is … |
|---|---|
| célibataire | single |
| divorcé(e) | divorced |
| fiancé(e) | engaged |
| marié(e) | married |
| mort(e) | dead |
| séparé(e) | separated |

Note that beau / belle mean 'step-' or '-in-law':
beau-père = stepfather
belle-mère = mother-in-law

## Worked example

READING   target B

Read Margaux's description of her family.

*Quand j'étais petite, j'habitais avec mes parents, mais ils sont séparés depuis quatre ans alors j'habite chez ma mère et mon beau-père. Mon beau-père a un fils qui n'habite plus chez nous depuis son mariage l'hiver dernier.*

*La plupart du temps j'ai de bons rapports avec ma mère. Quelquefois elle se fâche avec moi et elle m'énerve quand elle me pose tout le temps des questions. Elle ne me permet pas de sortir tard le soir, sauf pour aller aux cours de judo. Mon beau-père est sportif, il aime jouer au golf et je m'entends assez bien avec lui. De temps en temps il m'aide avec mes devoirs si j'ai des difficultés.*

Answer in English. Who does Margaux live with?   mum and stepdad

## Reading exam tips

• Comprehension questions on a reading passage usually follow the order of the text.

• Questions in English have to be answered in English – an answer given in French will be wrong, even if it is the correct French word.

This question requires a knowledge not of key words, but of grammar. It is in the **present** tense: Who does Margaux live with? So you must ignore references to the past j'habitais (I lived) and focus on maintenant (now): j'habite (I live).

## Now try this

READING   target B

Answer these questions on the text above.

1  Why does Margaux's stepbrother no longer live with them?
2  How does Margaux's mother annoy her?
3  What is the only thing Margaux can go out late for?
4  When does Margaux's stepfather help her with homework?

Read the questions carefully and give the answer which is being asked for, not the related words you can understand.

Write the exact detail – not just 'judo'.

# Friends

You may talk about friends in a speaking assessment, where you will need to ask AND answer questions. Make sure you know the question words!

## Les copains / copines

| | |
|---|---|
| ami (m) / amie (f) | friend |
| bavarder | to chat |
| mec (m) | guy, dude |
| charmant(e) | charming |
| (mé)content(e) | (dis)pleased, (un)satisfied |
| effronté(e) | cheeky |
| égoïste | selfish |
| insupportable | unbearable |
| (im)patient(e) | (im)patient |
| Je le / la connais depuis la maternelle. | I have known him / her since nursery school. |
| Mon meilleur ami / Ma meilleure amie s'appelle … | My best friend is called … |
| Il est le moins intéressant du groupe. | He is the least interesting in the group. |

### Question words

| | |
|---|---|
| qui | who |
| que | what |
| où | where |
| quand | when |
| quoi | what |
| quel(le) | which |
| qu'est-ce que / qui | what |
| pourquoi | why |
| combien de | how many / much |
| comment | how |
| à quelle heure | at what time |

Comment s'appelle votre ami?
What is your friend called?

Qu'est-ce que vous faites?
What do you do?

## Worked example

Décris ta photo.

> Ce garçon en pullover jaune s'appelle Hugo. Selon lui, il est champion de sport mais en vérité il passe tout son temps devant le petit écran. Il est le moins intéressant du groupe.

This student is accurate but in order to aim for a higher grade, he needs to use a variety of tenses and vocabulary.

**AIMING HIGHER**

> J'ai choisi de parler de mes copains, parce que ce sont les personnes les plus importantes dans ma vie. J'ai plusieurs amis dans ma classe, mais Marley est mon meilleur ami. C'est lui qui porte une casquette bleue sur la photo. C'est un mec très honnête et charmant et je peux tout lui dire. Cet été nous allons faire un stage de surf au pays de Galles et après avoir quitté le collège nous voudrions tous les deux aller en Australie pour travailler dans une école de surf.

The second student has included past, present, future and conditional tenses plus pronouns, different parts of the verb (je, nous, il) and a good variety of vocabulary.

**CONTROLLED ASSESSMENT**

Just because you don't make any mistakes, it doesn't necessarily mean you will score highly for accuracy. You need to use more complex language and your pronunciation and intonation must be generally good.

## Now try this

Describe a photo of your friends for about one minute. Include details of:

- names, ages, characteristics
- your opinion of them
- something you did in the past together
- something you are planning for the future.

# Hobbies

Do your research on hobbies BEFORE your writing assessment. Look up any words in advance and check you are confident in using them.

## Les passe-temps

| J'aime ... | I like ... |
|---|---|
| nager / danser | swimming / dancing |
| faire les magasins | shopping |
| jouer de la guitare | playing the guitar |
| jouer aux échecs | playing chess |
| aller au théâtre | going to the theatre |
| aller au club des jeunes | going to the youth club |
| tchater avec mes ami(e)s | chatting online with my friends |

### Likes and dislikes

Use these verbs with the infinitive to talk about your likes and dislikes: adorer, aimer, détester, préférer.

J'adore danser.
I love dancing (to dance).

Je déteste jouer de la batterie.
I hate playing the drums.

Je préfère rencontrer mes amis.
I prefer meeting my friends.

> Make sure you use the correct accents on Je préfère!

J'aime lire.    J'aime écouter de la musique.    J'aime regarder la télé.

## Worked example

Write about your hobbies.

J'aime écouter de la musique et regarder la télé. Le soir je tchate avec mes copains ou je joue en ligne. Je déteste faire mes devoirs, mais c'est nécessaire et je les fais sur Internet.

**AIMING HIGHER** Si j'ai le temps j'aime lire des livres, surtout des livres d'épouvante. J'ai lu tous les livres de Harry Potter et j'ai vu les films. Quand j'étais plus jeune je jouais du piano chaque soir, mais maintenant je préfère bavarder avec mes amis. Le weekend prochain nous irons à une fête de la musique et j'espère qu'il ne pleuvra pas parce qu'on va dormir sous des tentes.

> Use ou (or) and et (and) to list two activities, as this student has – but don't keep adding ou and et to make it into a long list. Try instead to use a variety of tenses and forms (je, il, etc.)!

> • Use si (if) and quand (when) to make sentences more interesting.
> • This student has also woven in **present** (what he likes), **perfect** (a book he has read), **imperfect** (what he used to do) and **future** (what he will do next weekend).

## Now try this

What do you do in your free time?
• Describe your likes and dislikes.
• Give details of a hobby you have done.
• Explain how your hobbies have changed.
• Write about your plans for next weekend.

> If your writing task has a series of bullet points or questions, like this one, you must answer them all. Likewise, your written work must be of a suitable length if you are aiming for a higher grade (at least 200 words).

# Sport

When talking about sports, make sure you get the du, de la, de l' and des parts correct.

## Faire du sport

| Je joue / jouais ... | I play / used to play ... |
|---|---|
| au basket / tennis | basketball / tennis |
| Je fais / faisais ... | I do / used to do ... |
| des arts martiaux | martial arts |
| du vélo | cycling |
| de la danse | dancing |
| de l'aérobic | aerobics |
| de l'aviron | rowing |
| de l'équitation | horseriding |
| de l'escalade | rock climbing |
| du patin à roulettes | rollerskating |
| de la voile | sailing |
| du ski nautique | waterskiing |
| des sports d'hiver | winter sports |
| une / deux fois par semaine | once / twice a week |
| tous les samedis | every Saturday |

### To play / do sports

- jouer + à + sport / game:
  Je joue au football.
  I play football.
  Je joue aux cartes.
  I play cards.

- faire + de with other sports:
  Je fais de la natation.   I swim.

Je fais du ski.     Je joue au rugby.

## Worked example

**READING**   **target B**

Read the text. Past, present or future?

> J'aime le sport. Quand j'étais petit je jouais au foot. Je m'entraînais deux fois par semaine et le weekend on jouait contre un autre club. Une fois on a gagné le championnat, c'était incroyable! Maintenant, mon sport préféré c'est le judo et j'en fais tous les jeudis. Cet été, pendant les grandes vacances, je vais faire du ski nautique pour la première fois. J'aimerais aussi faire du ski parce que je n'en ai jamais fait et je voudrais bien apprendre. **Paul, 16 ans**

Put a cross in the correct box.

|  | Past | Present | Future |
|---|---|---|---|
| Football | ☒ | ☐ | ☐ |

Use the example answer to see what you have to do. Here, you need to identify whether the English word given is referred to in the past, present or future, and put a cross in the correct box.

### Past, present and future

- For 'past' activities you need to look for words in the imperfect or perfect tense (étais, past participles).

- For 'present' you need present tense verbs with words such as maintenant (now) or d'habitude (usually).

- For 'future' look for the near future (je vais + infinitive), future tense (je ferai) or the conditional (je voudrais).

## Now try this

**READING**   **target B**

Did Paul do these activities in the past, present or future?

|  | Past | Present | Future |
|---|---|---|---|
| (a) Winning the championship | ☐ | ☐ | ☐ |
| (b) Doing a martial art | ☐ | ☐ | ☐ |
| (c) Waterskiing | ☐ | ☐ | ☐ |
| (d) Skiing | ☐ | ☐ | ☐ |

# Going out

Learning vocabulary is essential in preparing for your listening exam. Use the learning tips below!

## Sortir

| | |
|---|---|
| Tu veux sortir? | Do you want to go out? |
| Tu viens / Vous venez? | Are you coming? |
| Tu veux / Vous voulez …? | Do you want to …? |
| aller au cinéma | go to the cinema |
| aller à la piscine | go to the pool |
| aller au centre de loisirs | go to the leisure centre |
| faire du bowling | go bowling |
| faire une promenade | go for a walk |
| Je peux / Je ne peux pas. | I can / can't. |
| Je dois / Il me faut … | I have to … |
| promener le chien | walk the dog |
| garder mon petit frère | look after my little brother |
| faire mes devoirs | do my homework |
| ranger ma chambre | tidy my room |
| me relaxer | chill out |

### tu or vous

**FAMILIAR**

vous

tu = 'you' to another young person, family member / friend, animal

vous = 'you' plural of tu (more than one young person)

tu

**FORMAL**

vous = 'you' to adult(s), teacher(s), official(s)

Avoid tu or vous by using on:

On va au stade?

Do you want to go to the stadium?

## Worked example

🎧 6 | target E

Listen to the conversation and complete the two sentences with English words.

Léa is invited to the … cinema

She can't go as she has to … tidy her room.

— Salut Léa! On va au cinéma ce soir, tu veux venir?

— Oh non, je ne peux pas; je dois ranger ma chambre!

## Learning vocabulary

To prepare for your listening exam, you need to learn lots of vocabulary.

- LOOK at and learn the words.
- COVER the English words.
- WRITE the English words.
- LOOK at all the words.
- SEE how many you have got right.

For an extra challenge, cover the **French** words and repeat the stages above.

## Now try this

🎧 7 | target E

Listen to the rest of the recording and complete the sentences with the phrases in the box.

(a) Thomas is invited to go to …

(b) He can't go as he has to …

(c) Sarah is invited to go to the …

(d) She can't go as she has to …

| | | |
|---|---|---|
| the leisure centre | the restaurant | the swimming pool |
| do homework | look after someone | walk the dog |

# Weekends

Use the phrases on this page to say what you did last weekend.

## Le weekend

| | |
|---|---|
| J'ai fait la grasse matinée. | I slept in / had a lie-in. |
| Je suis sorti(e). | I went out. |
| Nous avons vu un film. | We saw a film. |
| Je suis allé(e) en ville. | I went to town. |
| Je me suis levé(e) à dix heures. | I got up at ten o'clock. |
| J'ai regardé (un match). | I watched (a match) |
| On s'est bien amusé(e)s. | We had a good time. |
| Je me suis cassé la jambe. | I broke my leg. |
| C'était marrant / génial. | It was funny / great. |
| Il faisait froid / chaud. | It was cold / hot. |
| Il y avait du monde. | Everybody was there. |

### Irregular participles (Pages 95–96)

J'ai …

| | |
|---|---|
| bu | drank |
| fait | did |
| écrit | wrote |
| lu | read |
| pris | took |
| reçu | received |
| vu | saw |

On a fait du VTT.

---

## Worked example — target C

Read the text and answer the question in English.

> Comme on n'avait pas cours vendredi dernier, nous avons décidé de faire du VTT. Il faisait beau et chaud et on est parti avec un pique-nique pour aller se baigner au lac. Malheureusement en rentrant, j'au eu un accident. Une voiture est sortie trop vite d'une ruelle et je me suis retrouvée à l'hôpital. J'ai passé le weekend au lit et maintenant j'ai la jambe dans le plâtre et je marche avec des béquilles.

Why did Zoë decide to go mountain biking?

As she didn't have lessons on Friday

## Reading rule

ALWAYS read the WHOLE text through first and get the sense of what happened. THEN look at the questions: do you need to understand every word in the text to answer them?

This question tells you what **VTT** means: mountain biking. It's up to you to work out the meaning of the other words nearby: **Comme on n'avait pas cours** (As we didn't have lessons).

- You can often deduce the meaning of unfamiliar words. They may look like English words: **l'hôpital** (hospital), or be familiar from other French words: **ruelle** (small street).
- Sometimes the context will give you the meaning. Here, Zoë has had an accident and damaged her leg which is in **plâtre** (similar to the word plaster) so **marche avec des béquilles** probably means 'walk on crutches'.

---

## Now try this — target C

Answer these questions on the text above in English.

1 What was the weather like?
2 Name **two** things they were planning to do at the lake.
3 Why did Zoë end up in hospital?
4 Name **two** consequences of her accident.

# TV programmes

If you talk about television, you need to be able to describe the TYPE of programmes you watch. Don't just give the names of programmes in English.

## La télévision

| | |
|---|---|
| actualités / informations (fpl) | news |
| comédie dramatique (f) | drama |
| comédie de situation (f) | sitcom |
| dessin animé (m) | cartoon |
| documentaire (m) | documentary |
| feuilleton (m) | soap |
| jeu télévisé (m) | game show |
| journal (télévisé) (m) | the news |
| météo (f) | weather forecast |
| policier (m) | detective programme |
| pub (f) | adverts |
| série (f) | series |
| télévision câblée (f) | cable television |
| télévision satellite (f) | satellite television |
| chaîne (de télévision) (f) | television channel |
| poste de télévision (m) | television set |
| télécommande (f) | remote control |

J'adore les dessins animés.

### Pronouncing préféré(e)

Préféré(e) is one of the worst pronounced words by students in the speaking assessment! Pull your lips into a smile and keep them there as you say all three syllables.

mon émission préférée
my favourite programme

Une de mes émissions préférées, c'est …
One of my favourite programmes is …

---

## Worked example

Qu'est-ce que tu aimes regarder à la télé?

Je n'aime pas tellement les jeux télévisés alors je n'en regarde jamais. Je déteste la pub parce que c'est toujours trop long.

This makes good use of the adverb **tellement** (much) and connective **alors** (so); the two negatives are accurate and the student justifies the reason for disliking adverts, using **parce que**.

**AIMING HIGHER** J'aime regarder les émissions amusantes et j'adore prendre mon petit déjeuner en regardant ma chaîne préférée. Récemment, j'ai regardé un super bon film qui s'appelle 'L'homme c'est elle', un film américain. Il s'agit d'une fille qui rêve de devenir footballeuse professionnelle. C'était génial!

This answer is more interesting as it uses adjectives (**amusantes, préférée**). It also uses the past tense (**j'ai regardé un super bon film**), and it gives the title in French, which avoids using English.

---

## Now try this

Prepare answers to these questions. Speak for about one minute.
- Quelle est votre émission préférée?
- Pourquoi regardez-vous la télévision?
- Qu'est-ce que vous avez regardé récemment?

# Cinema

Describing the last film you have seen is a useful topic for a speaking or writing assessment.

## Le cinéma

| | |
|---|---|
| acteur (m) / actrice (f) | actor |
| film d'aventures (m) | adventure film |
| film comique (m) | comedy |
| film d'espionnage (m) | spy film |
| film de science-fiction (m) | sci-fi film |
| film de suspense (m) | thriller |
| film romantique / d'amour (m) | romance |
| film principal (m) | feature film |
| réduction (f) | reduction |
| salle complète | sold out |
| séance (f) | showing |
| soir (m) | evening |
| les effets spéciaux (mpl) | special effects |
| vedette (f) | film star |
| énerver | to annoy |
| version originale (VO) (f) | original version |

## avoir expressions

| | |
|---|---|
| avoir faim / soif | to be hungry / thirsty |
| avoir raison / tort | to be right / wrong |
| avoir besoin de | to need |
| avoir peur | to be afraid |
| avoir l'air | to look (angry, sad, etc.) |
| avoir lieu | to take place |
| avoir envie (de) | to feel like (doing something) |

J'ai peur des films d'horreur. I am afraid of horror films.

## Worked example  🎧 8  target A

Cyril and Noëlle are deciding which film to go and see.

Which of the following sentences is true?

- They both want to watch the thriller.
- They have different feelings about watching the thriller. ✓

– Regarde, au Méliès, film de suspense, avec mon actrice préférée!
– Oui, mais elle m'énerve!

## EXAM ALERT!

Questions like this can be challenging. They require careful listening as you need to distinguish between **choices** and **opinions**.

Students have struggled with exam questions similar to this – **be prepared!**   Result Plus

There is one positive opinion, **actrice préférée** (favourite actress) but the question asks whether they **both** want to watch the thriller, so you need to listen to the negative opinion which follows: elle m'énerve (she annoys me). You can then tell they do **not both** want to watch the thriller.

## Now try this  🎧 9  target A

Listen to the whole dialogue. Cyril and Noëlle decide to see the romantic film. Why?

Put a cross in the **three** correct boxes.

A  Some friends recommended it. ☐
B  They say they like the actress who is in it. ☐
C  There are reduced prices at the cinema. ☐
D  The time is convenient. ☐
E  It's a feel-good film. ☐
F  It's a French film. ☐

Don't cross more than **three** boxes.

# Music

If you are writing about music, make sure you also include your opinion of the music and some personal recollections, to make your text more interesting.

## La musique

| | |
|---|---|
| Mon chanteur préféré / ma chanteuse préférée, c'est ... | My favourite singer is ... |
| J'écoute ... | I listen to ... |
| Je suis fana de ... | I'm a fan of ... |
| la musique pop / rock | pop / rock |
| la musique folk / jazz | folk / jazz |
| la musique classique | classical music |
| Je joue du piano / de la guitare. | I play the piano / guitar. |
| célébrité (f) | celebrity |
| chanson (f) | song |
| groupe (m) | group / band |
| musicien (m) / musicienne (f) | musician |
| orchestre (m) | orchestra |
| chanter | to sing |
| écouter la radio | to listen to the radio |
| télécharger | to download |

### 'this' and 'that' » Page 84

| | |
|---|---|
| ce soir-là | that evening |
| cette tournée-là | that tour |
| ces chansons-là | those songs |
| ce chanteur-ci | this singer (male) |
| cette musicienne-ci | this musician (female) |
| ces mélodies-ci | these tunes |

Ed Sheeran, c'est mon chanteur préféré.

## Worked example

Write about your favourite singer.

L'été dernier, avec mes amis, je suis allée voir Rihanna en concert. C'était fantastique et nous avons chanté et dansé pendant tout le concert. Elle était formidable sur scène et je n'oublierai jamais cette soirée-là.

This student used more than one tense, e.g. the perfect (je suis allée – I went) and the future (je n'oublierai jamais – I will never forget).

**AIMING HIGHER** Beyoncé est vraiment une de mes chanteuses préférées et ce serait mon rêve d'aller la voir en concert. D'origine américaine et née à Houston au Texas, elle est considérée comme la personne la plus influente dans le monde de la musique de la décennie 2000–2010. Son premier album solo Dangerously in Love est sorti en 2003. Il a été l'un des albums les plus vendus de l'année.

- The conditional phrase ce serait mon rêve de + verb (it would be my dream to) is useful in lots of topics.
- Note also the good command of superlatives: la personne la plus influente (the most influential person) and l'un des albums les plus vendus (one of the most sold albums).

## Now try this

Write about 200 words on your favourite music group or solo artist.

- Explain why you have chosen this person.
- Give some background details on him / her.
- List his / her key successes.

- Describe an occasion when you saw him / her live, or express your hopes to do so in the future.

# Online activities

This page will help you talk about some online activities when you are preparing a text about your hobbies.

## En ligne

tchater     to talk online
jouer à des jeux     to play games
visiter des forums   to visit chatrooms
aller sur mon site perso
to go on my own site
parler à mes amis
to talk to my friends
chercher des informations
to look for information
envoyer des e-mails
to send emails
faire des recherches
to do research
mettre des photos en ligne
to upload photos
regarder des émissions de télé
to watch TV programmes
sauvegarder de la musique
to store music
télécharger de la musique
to download music

### Present tense: irregular verbs

| | | | | |
|---|---|---|---|---|
| envoyer | to send | ➡ | j'envoie | I send |
| aller | to go | ➡ | je vais | I go |
| mettre en ligne | to upload | ➡ | je mets en ligne | I upload |
| s'appeler | to be called | ➡ | je m'appelle | I am called |
| se lever | to get up | ➡ | je me lève | I get up |

Je surfe sur Internet.     I surf the internet.

## Worked example 🎧 10   target F

What does this person use the internet for?
Put a cross in the correct box.

| | | | | |
|---|---|---|---|---|
| **A** playing games | ☐ | **D** downloading music | ☒ |
| **B** talking to friends | ☐ | **E** watching TV programmes | ☐ |
| **C** doing research | ☐ | **F** shopping | ☐ |

– Je télécharge de la musique.

- Look through the options A–F and remind yourself of any related **French** words before the recording plays.
- This type of activity is all about listening for **key** words – there are no opinions, alternatives or negatives.

## Now try this 🎧 11   target F

Listen to four more people and put a cross to note what they use the internet for.

| | A | B | C | D | E | F |
|---|---|---|---|---|---|---|
| 1 | | | | | | |
| 2 | | | | | | |
| 3 | | | | | | |
| 4 | | | | | | |

Don't make a silly mistake such as putting your cross in the wrong column.

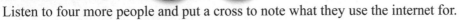

# Daily routine

To talk about daily routine, you will need to know times in the 12- AND 24-hour clock.

## Ma routine quotidienne

| Le matin / soir ... | In the morning / evening ... |
| --- | --- |
| L'après-midi ... | In the afternoon ... |
| À dix heures ... | At ten o'clock ... |
| je me lève | I get up |
| je me lave / je me douche | I wash / shower |
| je m'habille | I get dressed |
| je quitte la maison | I leave the house |
| je vais au collège | I go to school |
| je rentre à la maison | I return home |
| je dîne en famille | I have dinner with my family |
| je fais mes devoirs | I do my homework |
| je me couche | I go to bed |

### 12-hour clock

à = at

avant = before

après = after

For the 24-hour clock, see page 24.

| | | |
| --- | --- | --- |
| deux heures | deux heures cinq | deux heures et quart |
| deux heures et demie | trois heures moins le quart | trois heures moins dix |

---

**Worked example**

Read about Nina's daily routine.

> Les jours d'école, le matin, je me lève à sept heures et je me douche immédiatement. Dix minutes plus tard, je m'habille vite. Je mange une tartine avec du miel et je bois un chocolat chaud avant de quitter la maison à sept heures et demie. Mon frère et moi, nous allons au collège en vélo, mais j'y vais avec mes copines et lui avec ses copains. On n'y va jamais ensemble. S'il pleut, nous prenons le car de ramassage qui passe à sept heures vingt. À midi nous mangeons à la cantine et le soir nous dînons avec nos parents, puis nous faisons nos devoirs et je tchate en ligne avec ma copine. Nous nous couchons à neuf heures et demie.

Put a cross in the correct box.
At ten past seven Nina ...

**A** gets up ☐   **B** showers ☐   **C** gets dressed ☒

### Multiple-choice questions

- In multiple-choice questions, you really do have to understand all the text so as not to get misled.
- Here, all the items in the choices are in the text, but you have to work out the meaning behind them in order to get the correct answer.

---

**Now try this**

Be careful: car = coach

Put a cross in the correct box to complete each sentence.

1 Nina has breakfast ...
  **A** at half past seven ☐
  **B** on her way to school ☐
  **C** before leaving home ☐

2 She cycles to school ...
  **A** with her friends ☐
  **B** with her brother and his friends ☐
  **C** alone ☐

3 On a wet day she leaves for school ...
  **A** at seven o'clock ☐
  **B** at twenty past seven ☐
  **C** in the car ☐

4 In the evening Nina's brother
  **A** chats to his friend online ☐
  **B** does homework with his parents ☐
  **C** does homework ☐

# Breakfast time

This page will help you talk about breakfast in the present and in the past.

## Le petit déj(euner)

| Pour le petit déj je bois ... | For breakfast I drink ... |
|---|---|
| du thé | tea |
| du café | coffee |
| du jus d'orange | orange juice |
| du chocolat chaud | hot chocolate |
| Je ne bois pas de lait. | I don't drink milk. |
| Je mange ... | I eat ... |
| des céréales (fpl) | cereals |
| des crêpes (fpl) | pancakes |
| des petits pains (mpl) | bread rolls |
| un croissant | a croissant |
| une tartine | a slice of bread and butter |
| de la confiture | jam |
| du miel | honey |
| un œuf | an egg |
| du jambon | ham |
| Je ne mange rien. | I don't eat anything. |
| Je suis pressé(e). | I am in a hurry. |

### Before and after

- avant de + infinitive = before doing something

  Avant d'aller au collège je mange des toasts.
  Before going to school I eat some toast.

- après avoir + past participle = after having done something

  Après avoir mangé mon petit déj je suis allé au collège.
  After having eaten breakfast I went to school.

J'adore les céréales.

---

## Worked example

Qu'est-ce que tu as mangé pour ton petit déjeuner?

Pour le petit déjeuner je mange des céréales avec du lait et je bois un jus d'orange.

Ce matin j'ai mangé des céréales et une tartine beurrée avec de la confiture à la framboise. Le weekend, si on a du temps, on fait des crêpes. J'adore ça. Je les mange avec du sucre mais ma sœur les préfère avec des tranches de banane et du miel et avec tout ça de la crème fraîche! Je trouve ça dégoûtant!

## Aiming higher

Four ways to improve your answers:

1. Add an OPINION: C'est assez ennuyeux mais vraiment important. (It's quite boring but really important.)

2. Include a TIME EXPRESSION: toujours (always), quelquefois (sometimes), de temps en temps (now and again).

3. Add a CONDITIONAL: Le petit déjeuner de mes rêves serait ... (The breakfast of my dreams would be ...).

4. Use the PLUPERFECT: Hier je me sentais malade parce que je n'avais rien mangé avant d'aller à l'école. (Yesterday I felt ill because I had not eaten before I went to school.)

---

## Now try this

Use points 1–4 above to prepare answers to these questions.

- Qu'est-ce que serait le petit déjeuner de vos rêves?
- Qu'est-ce que vous mangez / buvez pour le petit déjeuner?
- Selon vous, c'est important, le petit déjeuner?

# Eating at home

When writing about the meals you have at home, remember to make your sentences longer by adding a connective. A connective is a word that joins two sentences together.

## Manger à la maison

| | |
|---|---|
| casse-croûte (m) | snack |
| dîner (m) | dinner |
| fait maison | home-made |
| repas du soir (m) | evening meal |
| salle à manger (f) | dining room |
| plat cuisiné (m) | ready meal |
| plateau (m) | tray |
| pomme de terre (f) | potato |
| souper (m) | supper / dinner |
| steak-haché (m) | minced beef / hamburger |
| viande (f) | meat |
| J'ai trop mangé. | I am full. |

de la salade

des frites     de la viande

## Worked example

WRITING

Write about what you normally eat at home.

Mon casse-croûte préféré c'est le croque-monsieur. C'est un sandwich grillé. Je le fais moi-même. On fait un sandwich avec du jambon et du fromage puis on le fait griller. Je le mange avec du ketchup!

**AIMING HIGHER**

Chez nous, on mange quand on a faim! Par exemple, hier ma sœur a mangé du steak-haché avec des pommes de terre à quatre heures en rentrant de l'école, mais moi, je suis allé à mon club alors je ne suis pas arrivé à la maison avant cinq heures et demie et il ne restait plus rien dans le frigo. Donc j'ai dû manger un plat cuisiné du congélateur parce que mes parents n'étaient pas allés au supermarché.

**CONTROLLED ASSESSMENT**

Stick to the 200-word limit. Students who write less than this may be penalised, and students who write much more than this often introduce mistakes.

This is a good response but to get a higher grade it would need to use more than one tense.

This response deserves a higher grade because it uses **connectives** such as quand, avec, donc, parce que. It also includes the **perfect** tense of a modal verb (j'ai dû manger) and an **imperfect** tense (il ne restait plus rien), as well as the present tense and a variety of structures.

## Now try this

WRITING

Write 100 words about your eating habits at home.

- Vous mangez en famille le soir?
- Qu'est-ce que vous aimez manger le plus?
- Qui fait la cuisine chez vous?
- Décrivez votre repas idéal.

Here are some connectives you could use:

| | | | |
|---|---|---|---|
| et | and | parce que | because |
| ou | or | (même) si | (even) if |
| mais | but | alors | then |
| donc | so / therefore | aussi | also |
| car | because | quand | when |

# Healthy eating

Learn some key phrases from this page to talk about healthy eating.

## La santé alimentaire

| | |
|---|---|
| allégé(e) | low-fat |
| en forme | fit |
| équilibré(e) | balanced |
| garder la forme | to keep fit |
| boissons sucrées (fpl) | sugary drinks |
| bon pour la santé | good for your health |
| mauvais pour la santé | bad for your health |
| gras(se) | fatty, greasy |
| malsain(e) | unhealthy |
| nourriture bio (f) | organic food |
| perdre du poids | to lose weight |
| prendre du poids | to put on weight |
| faire un régime | to be on a diet |
| résister à la tentation | to resist temptation |
| sucreries (fpl) | sweet things |
| végétarien(ne) | vegetarian |

## Present tense: -ir verbs   ≫ Page 90

- grossir    to put on weight

| | |
|---|---|
| je grossis | nous grossissons |
| tu grossis | vous grossissez |
| il / elle / on grossit | ils / elles grossissent |

- choisir    to choose
- finir    to finish
- maigrir    to lose weight

Je choisis de la salade.   I choose salad.

Je choisis des légumes.

## Worked example   READING   target C

Read this conversation.

**Gisèle** J'aime manger des sucreries, mais je joue au volley au moins une fois par semaine, alors je ne grossis pas.

**Théo** La nourriture est la chose la plus importante. Je mange beaucoup de salades, de légumes … Je suis végétarien depuis trois ans.

**Rémi** À mon avis on doit s'hydrater. J'ai toujours une bouteille d'eau avec moi pour éviter les boissons sucrées.

**Jean** J'ai de la chance, parce que je peux manger et boire tout ce que je veux sans prendre du poids. Le sport n'a aucune importance pour moi.

Who makes the following statement?

I don't eat meat. Théo

- Théo doesn't say Je ne mange pas de viande (I don't eat meat), but he does say Je suis végétarien which means the same thing.
- You are not looking for direct translations in this kind of task, but the same meaning phrased differently.

## Aiming higher

Look online for forums and articles about any of the subjects you are revising – see how much you can understand of authentic texts to give you confidence in the reading exam.

## Now try this   READING   target C

Who makes the following statements?

**(a)** I avoid unhealthy drinks.    **(b)** I don't need to exercise.    **(c)** I have a sweet tooth.

# Health problems

You may well come across some vocabulary about health problems in your listening or reading exams, so learn it carefully.

## Problèmes de santé

| | |
|---|---|
| alcool (m) | alcohol |
| aller mieux | to feel better |
| arrêter de fumer | to stop smoking |
| avoir la grippe | to have flu |
| blesser | to injure |
| blessure (f) | injury |
| cassé(e) | broken |
| dormir | to sleep |
| en bonne santé | healthy |
| fatigué(e) | tired |
| fumeur (m) / fumeuse (f) | smoker |
| garder le lit | to stay in bed |
| médecin (m) | doctor |
| obésité (f) | obesity |
| premiers secours (mpl) | first aid |
| prendre un médicament | to take medicine |
| se casser | to break (bone) |
| se sentir | to feel |
| tousser | to cough |

### Saying what hurts
### J'ai mal ...

à l'épaule
au doigt
à l'estomac
au bras
à la tête
au dos
à la jambe
au pied
aux dents
à la gorge

Je me suis fait mal à la main.
I hurt my hand.
J'ai mal au genou.   My knee hurts.

---

## Worked example

LISTENING 12   target A

**Habits and health**

Alain is talking about his health.

Put a cross in the box by the person the statement refers to.

Alain ☒   Freya ☐   Grandad ☐

I can't stop smoking.

– Je fume depuis cinq ans. Je m'y suis habitué et … ben … j'ai essayé plusieurs fois d'arrêter mais je ne réussis jamais.

- Read the **title** and the **rubric** before you listen – here you can get one step ahead by knowing the extract is going to be on the subject of habits and health, and involves three characters.
- The start of the text is all in the 'I' form, **je**, and you already know that Alain is doing the talking, so the statement refers to himself.

---

## Now try this

LISTENING 13   target A

Listen to the whole extract. Who does each statement refer to: Alain, Freya or Grandad?

**(a)** I am often ill.

**(b)** I think cigarettes are damaging my health.

**(c)** I am totally against smoking.

**(d)** I will never smoke in front of my family.

# Visitor information

You need to know the vocabulary for places in a town. Learn the genders, too!

## À l'office de tourisme

| | |
|---|---|
| bibliothèque (f) | library |
| bowling (m) | bowling alley |
| centre sportif (m) | sports centre |
| gare routière (f) | coach station |
| hypermarché (m) | hypermarket |
| jardin public / parc (m) | park |
| magasins / commerces (mpl) | shops |
| marché (m) | market |
| parking (m) | car park |
| patinoire (f) | ice rink |
| piscine (f) | swimming pool |
| place (f) | square |
| stade (m) | stadium |
| supermarché (m) | supermarket |
| théâtre (m) | theatre |
| toilettes (fpl) | toilets |
| région (f) | local area / region |

## Saying 'the'

| masc | fem | plural |
|---|---|---|
| le | la | les |

le and la = l' before a vowel or silent h:

l'église   the church

l'hôpital   the hospital

Le marché est situé dans la rue du Palais.
The market is on Palace Steet.

Les magasins sont affreux.
The shops are awful.

La gare routière se trouve en centre-ville.
The coach station is in the town centre.

---

## Worked example

Write about what your home town is like.

Grondville est assez petite mais il y a un grand parc où je joue au football avec mes copains le weekend. Pour les sportifs, il y a aussi le bowling et la piscine. Malheureusement la patinoire est fermée depuis trois ans.

**AIMING HIGHER**  À Grondville il n'y a pas d'hypermarché mais il y a un marché qui est situé sur la place du Vieux Marché, où l'on vend des produits régionaux. Grondville est un centre agricole célèbre pour des produits laitiers comme le fromage bleu, et pour des fruits, noix et légumes selon la saison. Je vous recommanderais de visiter la ville.

## Using English words

Students who use lots of **cognates** (words which are the same in English) will only sound impressive if they pronounce them in the correct French way. Filling a presentation with English words is **not** a good idea.

Malheureusement (unfortunately) is an effective way of offering an opinion.

- There is good use of a negative il n'y a pas + de (there is not) and the opposite il y a un / une (there is a).
- Notice the detail about the town and the good use of adjective agreements, for example des produits régionaux (regional products).
- The use of the conditional sentence Je vous recommanderais de visiter la ville (I would recommend that you visit the town) helps aim for a higher grade.

---

## Now try this

Write 100 words about what there is and isn't in your (nearest) town.

Adapt the examples above for **your** town.

# Things to do in town

This page gives you more town vocabulary to help with listening and reading tasks.

## Activités en ville

| | |
|---|---|
| Il y a un / une ... | There is a ... |
| Il n'y a pas de ... | There isn't a ... |
| boulangerie / boucherie (f) | baker's / butcher's |
| bureau des objets trouvés (m) | lost property office |
| cathédrale (f) | cathedral |
| château (m) | castle |
| gare SNCF (f) | railway station |
| hôtel de ville (m) / mairie (f) | town hall |
| jardin zoologique (m) | zoo |
| monument (m) | monument |
| musée (m) | museum |
| palais (m) | palace |
| plage (f) | beach |

### Saying 'a', 'an' and 'some' » Page 80

| masc | fem | plural |
|---|---|---|
| un | une | des |

Il y a un château.    There is a castle.

Il y a une gare SNCF.
There is a railway station. ✓

Il y a des musées.
There are (some) museums. ✓

- After a negative, un and une = de
  Mais il n'y a pas de cathédrale.
  But there isn't a cathedral. ✗

---

## Worked example — READING — target F

Read the information from a notice board.

| A | B |
|---|---|
| **Château-musée**<br>**Fermé le dimanche**<br>**et le lundi** | **Gare SNCF**<br>**Tournez à gauche** |

| C | D |
|---|---|
| **Office de**<br>**tourisme**<br>**17 rue Jean**<br>**Jaurès** | Il y a une plage à 200 mètres |

| E | F |
|---|---|
| **Jardin zoologique**<br>**à un kilomètre** | **Bureau des**<br>**objets trouvés**<br>**15 rue de**<br>**Château** |

Where should Olga go to sunbathe? D

## EXAM ALERT!

Students scored very well in this question, with a large number gaining full marks. A mastery of basic vocabulary items and a degree of deductive reasoning are required in such tasks.

This was a real exam question that a lot of students struggled with – be prepared! | ResultsPlus

## Reading strategies

- Focus on the vocabulary of places which you need in order to identify where the people should go.
- If you have revised vocabulary, you might know that la plage = beach. It is not a word that looks anything like the English, so if you don't know it, answer the other questions first and then come back to it and see which options remain.

---

## Now try this — READING — target F

Where should these people go, according to the information above?

**(a)** Jean-Yves wants to get a plan of the town.

**(b)** Marion wants to see some animals.

**(c)** Anne needs to catch a train.

**(d)** Khaled has lost his mobile phone.

# Signs around town

Look carefully at the vocabulary on this page, as signs in a town may crop up in reading questions.

## Les panneaux en ville

| | |
|---|---|
| affiche (f) | poster |
| défense de | forbidden to |
| interdit de | forbidden to |
| il est recommandé de | it is recommended to |
| en avance | in advance |
| entrée (f) | entrance |
| sortie (de secours) (f) | (emergency) exit |
| inclus | included |
| bienvenue ouvert | welcome open |
| désolé fermé | sorry closed |
| distributeur de billets (m) | cash dispenser |
| municipal(e) | public / municipal |
| visite guidée (f) | guided tour |
| zone piétonne (f) | pedestrian zone |
| heures d'ouverture (fpl) | opening hours |
| vacances d'hiver (fpl) | winter holidays |

## Days of the week

Days in French always have a lower case letter to start.

| | |
|---|---|
| lundi | jeudi |
| mardi | vendredi |
| mercredi | samedi |
| | dimanche |

| | |
|---|---|
| tous les samedis | every Saturday |
| le samedi | on Saturday(s) |
| sauf le lundi | except Monday |
| de mardi à vendredi | from Tuesday to Friday |
| les jours fériés | public holidays |

## Worked example

READING    target **E**

Read these signs.

A **Bibliothèque municipale ouverte: 9h – 18h**

B **Défense de fumer dans la zone piétonne**

C Coiffeur Martin Ouvert tous les jours sauf le dimanche

D **Concert au Palais** Il est recommandé d'acheter les billets à l'avance.

E **Boulangerie italienne Fermé pour les vacances d'hiver**

jeter = to throw
fumer = to smoke

Choose the correct answer.

You can't **smoke** / go on Sundays / throw things in the pedestrian zone.

- Here, you need to locate the correct **sign** and then the correct **message** contained in that sign. The question mentions pedestrian zone so it is easy to spot that the sign you need is B, as it has the cognate la **zone piétonne**.
- Now you only need to work out what the verb fumer means.

## Now try this

READING    target **E**

Choose the correct answers, using the information on the signs above.

1 The **bakery / library / concert hall** is closed for the holidays.

2 You should buy concert tickets **in advance / online / from the ticket office**.

3 You can't get your hair cut on **Friday / Monday / Sunday**.

# Travelling by train

The 24-hour clock is used a lot in France, especially for opening times and on train timetables, so check you are confident with numbers up to cinquante-neuf (59).

## Voyager en train

| | |
|---|---|
| aller-retour (m) | return ticket |
| aller-simple (m) | single ticket |
| arrivée (f) | arrival |
| billet (m) | ticket |
| carnet (m) | book of tickets |
| chemin de fer (m) | railway |
| compartiment (m) | compartment |
| consigne (f) | left luggage |
| contrôleur (m) | ticket inspector |
| départ (m) | departure |
| destination (f) | destination |
| guichet (m) | ticket office |
| horaire (m) | timetable |
| quai (m) | platform |
| supplément (m) | supplement |
| tarif (m) | fare |
| wagon-lit (m) | sleeper |
| wagon-restaurant (m) | restaurant car |

### 24-hour clock

Page 104

The 24-hour clock is easy if you know your numbers!

It is used for opening times, train times or the time an event is taking place.

**09:30** neuf heures trente

**12:45** douze heures quarante-cinq

**16:15** seize heures quinze

**20:40** vingt heures quarante

**23:00** vingt-trois heures

Add the word **heures** between the hour and the minutes to show 'o'clock'.

à = at: à vingt heures (at 20.00 hours).

de ... à = from ... to

vers 21h30 = around 21.30

---

## Worked example    LISTENING 14    target E

(a) Listen and note the departure and arrival times of the train. 14h37 / 17h18

(b) What other detail is given about this train? book tickets in advance

- Le TGV pour Paris part à 14h37.
- Il arrive à quelle heure?
- Il arrive à 17h18. Il faut réserver les billets à l'avance.

TGV = train à grande vitesse (high-speed train)

Don't rush to write 10 every time you hear **dix** – wait and see if it is attached to another number, for example **dix-sept** which makes it 17.

## EXAM ALERT!

Make sure you are really familiar with numbers and practise them in a variety of contexts.

Don't muddle similar numbers such as **trente** (30) and **treize** (13) or **quatre** (4) and **quatorze** (14).

Students have struggled with exam questions similar to this – **be prepared!**    ResultsPlus

---

## Now try this    LISTENING 15    target E

Listen to the next three dialogues at the station and for each one note:

(a) the departure time          (b) the arrival time          (c) one further detail

# Weather

Try to add a weather phrase to your written or spoken assessments, in a variety of tenses.

## La météo

il pleut     il neige     il fait du soleil

il y a du brouillard     il fait froid     il fait chaud

| | |
|---|---|
| chaleur (f) | heat |
| ciel (m) | sky |
| éclaircie (f) | sunny interval |
| nuage (m) | cloud |
| orage (m) | thunderstorm |
| pluie (f) | rain |
| vent (m) | wind |
| couvert | overcast |
| ensoleillé | sunny |

### Different tenses

PRESENT:
| | |
|---|---|
| Il y a du vent. | It is windy. |
| Il fait chaud. | It is hot. |

PAST (IMPERFECT):
| | |
|---|---|
| Il y avait du vent. | It was windy. |
| Il faisait chaud. | It was hot. |

FUTURE:
| | |
|---|---|
| Il y aura du vent. | It will be windy. |
| Il fera chaud. | It will be hot. |
| Il va pleuvoir. | It's going to rain. |

CONDITIONAL:
| | |
|---|---|
| Il y aurait du vent. | It would be windy. |
| Il ferait chaud. | It would be hot. |

## Worked example

READING    target C

Read the weather report and answer the question below.

Hier il faisait froid et il y avait du brouillard, mais aujourd'hui dans l'ouest, il fait du soleil et la température est de 15–19 degrés. Dans l'est c'est aussi ensoleillé et il n'y a pas de pluie. L'après-midi les nuages arriveront du nord et il y aura du vent partout. Pendant la nuit on risquera d'avoir des orages, surtout dans le nord. Demain la matinée sera caractérisée par des vents forts mais l'après-midi il y aura des éclaircies et il fera moins froid.

| | | |
|---|---|---|
| **lundi** |  | nuageux et froid |
| **mardi** | | froid avec de la pluie |
| **mercredi** |  | ensoleillé |

- Use your knowledge of **tenses** to help you answer this question – you are looking for past tense markers, such as **hier** (yesterday), or past tense verbs, such as **faisait** (was).
- Next, look for a mention of rain (**pluie / il pleut**). If you can't find those words, you know there was no rain yesterday.
- Remember:
  est (m) = east    nord (m) = north
  ouest (m) = west    sud (m) = south

True or false? It rained yesterday.    False

## Now try this

READING    target C

Put a cross by the **four** correct statements, according to the forecast above.

A It was foggy yesterday. ☐

B It is overcast in the west today. ☐

C There is no rain in the east. ☐

D There will be storms in the afternoon. ☐

E It might snow during the night. ☐

F Tomorrow morning will be windy. ☐

G It will be stormy on Tuesday. ☐

H The best day of the week is Wednesday. ☐

# Places in town

Make sure you can talk about places in town in the singular AND plural forms.

## En ville

| | |
|---|---|
| galerie d'art (f) | art gallery |
| banque (f) | bank |
| bar (m) | bar |
| café (m) | café |
| centre commercial (m) | shopping centre |
| centre de loisirs (m) | leisure centre |
| commissariat (m) | police station |
| discothèque / disco (f) | disco |
| espace vert (m) | park / green space |
| grand magasin (m) | department store |
| hôpital (m) | hospital |
| mosquée (f) | mosque |
| office de tourisme (m) | tourist office |
| quartier (m) | area (of town) |
| site touristique (m) | tourist attraction |
| spectacle (m) | show |
| propre | clean |
| tranquille | quiet |

## Singular and plural

Page 79

Il y a une piscine municipale.
There is a (one) public swimming pool.

Il y a plusieurs piscines.
There are several swimming pools.

Les piscines sont fantastiques.
The swimming pools are great.

* Nouns and adjectives ending -al / -au / -eau: plural = -x

| | singular | plural |
|---|---|---|
| animal | un animal | des animaux |
| office | un bureau | des bureaux |

## Worked example

WRITING

Write about your home town.

Newtown est une grande ville dans l'ouest de l'Angleterre. Il y a une grande zone piétonne avec plusieurs magasins et restaurants, mais il n'y a pas de sites touristiques. J'aime bien vivre ici parce que c'est tranquille et propre.

AIMING HIGHER

Quand vous visiterez ma ville l'année prochaine, vous y trouverez beaucoup de cafés et restaurants, où on peut manger des pizzas, des pâtes ou du curry. Si vous n'aimez pas faire des achats, il y a plein d'autres choses à faire. Par exemple, à côté du centre-ville, se trouve mon centre de loisirs favori qui a un mur d'escalade. Le weekend, mes copines et moi, on se retrouve souvent là-bas et on s'y amuse bien.

This student restricts himself to the **present** tense – he should have looked for a way of introducing a different tense, such as the **future** tense at the end: Le weekend prochain il y aura un grand spectacle dans l'espace vert et j'irai avec mes copains.

* This student has launched in with the **future** tense – this will create a good first impression. She then continues in the present tense but uses **interesting vocabulary and structures**, including relative pronouns and prepositions.
* Note also the different parts of the verb she uses: **vous, on, mes copains**. This improves the answer.

## Now try this

WRITING

Write 100 words to tell a visitor what they can do in your town when they come to visit you next year.

# Opinions of where you live

Using modifiers and adjectives in your speaking and writing will help improve your answers.

## Des opinions d'où tu habites

| | |
|---|---|
| J'aime vivre ici. | I like living here. |
| C'est une grande ville bruyante. | It is a large noisy town. |
| On peut faire des achats. | You can go shopping. |
| Les magasins sont assez chers. | The shops are quite expensive. |
| Il y a un beau jardin public. | There is a beautiful park. |
| Il y a beaucoup de choses à faire. | There are a lot of things to do. |
| Autrefois on pouvait aller à la piscine. | You used to be able to go to the swimming pool. |
| Aujourd'hui il n'y a rien à faire. | Today there is nothing to do. |
| C'est un endroit tranquille et ennuyeux. | It is a quiet and boring area. |
| Il y a trop de circulation. | There is too much traffic. |

### Modifiers

| | |
|---|---|
| assez | quite |
| beaucoup | much |
| trop | too (much) |
| encore | more |
| un peu | a bit |
| très | very |
| plus | more |
| moins | less |
| plutôt | rather |
| vraiment | really |
| Ma ville est très polluée. | My town is very polluted. |
| Le centre-ville est trop bruyant. | The town centre is too noisy. |

## Worked example

*WRITING*

What are the advantages and disadvantages of your local town?

J'aime habiter ici parce que c'est pittoresque, il n'y a pas beaucoup de circulation et il y a beaucoup de choses à faire et en plus, tous mes amis habitent ici.

**AIMING HIGHER**

Avant, ma ville était défavorisée et il n'y avait rien à faire. Cependant, il y a cinq ans on a investi beaucoup d'argent. De nos jours, l'avantage de ma ville, c'est qu'on peut y faire beaucoup de sports, aller au cinéma et fréquenter des sites touristiques. Mais l'inconvénient, c'est que tout ça coûte cher. Dans ma ville idéale, toutes les distractions seraient gratuites pour les ados et on pourrait aller au centre de loisirs sans payer.

- Avoid over-using the constructions **il y a** (there is / are) and **et** (and) to join sentences.

J'aime habiter ici.

- This answer uses a variety of structures and includes conditional phrases at the end: **serait gratuites** (would be free) and **on pourrait** (you could).

## Now try this

*WRITING*

Write 150 words about the advantages and disadvantages of where you live.

# Describing a town

This page will help you use modal verbs correctly in your town description.

## Description d'une ville

| | |
|---|---|
| banlieue (f) | suburb |
| bâtiment (m) | building |
| boîte de nuit (f) | nightclub |
| déchets (mpl) | rubbish |
| département (m) | administrative district |
| embouteillage (m) | traffic jam |
| endroit (m) | place |
| fleurs (fpl) | flowers |
| historique / | historic / |
| moderne | modern |
| industriel(le) | industrial |
| pittoresque | picturesque |
| touristique | touristy |

## Modal verbs

Page 93

Modal verbs are followed by another verb in the infinitive.

| | |
|---|---|
| pouvoir | to be able to |
| vouloir | to want to |
| devoir | to have to / should |

On ne peut pas interdire les voitures.
You can't ban cars.

On devrait installer des bancs.
You should install benches.

Je voudrais avoir un cinéma de 8 salles.
I would like to have an 8-screen cinema.

Il y a des fleurs partout.
There are flowers everywhere.

## Worked example

LISTENING 16   target A*

Fadela is talking about how her town could be improved. Answer the question by putting a cross in the correct box.

What would make the town centre nicer?

A. Have benches for people to sit on. ☒

B Have flowers everywhere. ☐

C Clean up the streets. ☐

– La ville est assez propre, on trouve très peu de déchets et de graffiti. Il y a des fleurs partout mais on devrait installer des bancs.

## EXAM ALERT!

This task proved tricky as it required an ability to distinguish between choices and to understand detail in the use of qualifiers, negatives and tenses.

This was a real exam question that a lot of students struggled with – be prepared!

ResultsPlus

- All three items in the answers are mentioned but you have to work out the meaning behind them all to narrow the answer to A.
- Using powers of deduction to help you, you can work out it can't be B (because there are flowers everywhere) and it can't be C (the town is quite clean and free from rubbish / graffiti).

## Now try this

LISTENING 17   target A*

Listen to the rest of the recording and choose the correct answers.

1 What does Fadela suggest to encourage more people to go to the shopping centre?

A More shops open on Sunday.   B Shops organise more events.   C Shops open later.

2 How could the traffic problem be solved? They should …

A ban cars from town centre.   B make parking more expensive.   C encourage parking outside town centre.

3 What would encourage young people to come to town?

A Build a sports centre.   B More activities for young people.   C Reduce prices of activities.

# Holiday destinations

When talking about holidays, it is crucial that you can say accurately where you are going.

## Où on va en vacances

| | |
|---|---|
| Je vais en Espagne / France. | I go to France / Spain. |
| Je suis allé(e) ... | I went ... |
| dans l'étranger | abroad |
| dans une station de ski | to a ski resort |
| dans une station balnéaire | to a beach resort |
| sur la côte | to the coast |
| au bord de la mer | to the seaside |
| bois (m) | wood |
| colline (f) | hill |
| ferme (f) | farm |
| lac (m) | lake |
| montagne (f) | mountain |
| pays (m) | country |
| rivière (f) | river |
| C'est près de Nantes. | It's near Nantes. |
| C'est loin de la côte. | It's far from the coast. |

## How to say 'to'

| masc | fem | plural |
|---|---|---|
| au or à l' | à la or à l' | aux |

Je suis allé(e) au bord de la mer.

J'adore passer les vacances au bord de la mer.
I love spending the holidays by the sea.

Je suis allé(e) à l'étranger.
I went abroad.

J'aime passer les vacances à la campagne.
I like holidaying in the country.

à + town      à Paris = to / in Paris
en + country  en Angleterre = to / in England

---

## Worked example

READING    target B

Read the text.

*Je m'appelle Célia et cette année je vais passer les vacances chez mes grands-parents qui habitent une ferme à la campagne parce que mes parents travaillent. Ma copine, Murielle va aller avec toute sa famille au camping la Forêt, au Lavandou. C'est une station balnéaire dans le Midi près de St Tropez.*
*Le père de mon cousin Rayan insiste toujours pour aller dans les Alpes, c'est à dire qu'il doit faire beaucoup de randonnées ou de VTT.*

Célia, Murielle or Rayan?

Who is going to stay with relatives? **Célia**

## EXAM ALERT!

This tests the ability to read a short text and identify which characters in it do particular things. It involves deductive reasoning and knowledge of a varied vocabulary.

In this sort of activity, the questions do not necessarily follow the order of the extract.

This was a real exam question that a lot of students struggled with – **be prepared!**    Results Plus

You have three names to choose from and each one of them mentions relatives connected in some way with holiday plans – père, famille, grands-parents, cousin – but only one of them is actually staying with relatives: **chez mes grands-parents**.

---

## Now try this

READING    target B

Célia, Murielle or Rayan?

(a) Who does not go on holiday with their parents?

(b) Who is going on a seaside holiday?

(c) Who will do mountain biking?

(d) Who will spend their holiday in a tent?

(e) Whose parents don't go on holiday?

# Accommodation

Use different tenses when talking about holidays, to aim for a higher grade.

## Le logement

| | |
|---|---|
| héberger / loger | to accommodate |
| réserver | to book |
| appartement loué (m) | rented flat |
| auberge de jeunesse (f) | youth hostel |
| chambre d'hôte (f) | bed and breakfast |
| gîte (m) | holiday home |
| hôtel (m) | hotel |
| chez des copains | at friends' house |
| confortable / complet | comfortable / full |
| spacieux / euse | spacious |
| en été | in summer |
| en hiver | in winter |
| en automne | autumn |
| au printemps | in spring |

aller voir = to visit (person)
visiter = to visit (place)

### Aiming higher

Use tense markers together with a range of tenses to aim for a higher grade.

✓ PRESENT

| | |
|---|---|
| toujours | always |
| d'habitude | usually |

Cette année on va dans un camping.
We are going to a campsite this year.

✓ PAST

| | |
|---|---|
| il y a longtemps | a long time ago |
| l'été précédent | the previous summer |

Avant on louait un gîte.
Before we used to rent a holiday home.

✓ FUTURE

| | |
|---|---|
| l'année prochaine | next year |
| dans quelques semaines | in a few weeks' time |

À l'avenir je réserverai une chambre à l'avance.
In future I will reserve a room in advance.

## Worked example

Write about your holidays,

D'habitude on loue un appartement dans une grande résidence avec piscine et salle de jeux, mais l'été dernier on est resté chez des copains à la montagne et cela a été un désastre.

**AIMING HIGHER**

Cet été, pour la première fois je resterai chez moi. Normalement je vais en vacances avec ma famille, mais l'année dernière j'ai décidé de ne plus le faire parce que mon petit frère m'énervait trop. Alors j'ai trouvé un petit emploi dans un restaurant où je travaillerai pendant la saison pour gagner de l'argent. À la fin des vacances, j'espère aller voir ma copine en Italie, toute seule!

These sentences hang together well with the present tense markers flowing on to the past tense, introduced very naturally by the expression **mais l'été dernier** (but last summer) + an opinion. A sound piece of writing.

- This text deserves a higher grade as it flows well and uses a variety of tenses + tense markers.
- It also includes some interesting structures: **espérer** + infinitive (to hope to), **pour** + infinitive (in order to) and **toute seule** (all alone) with the correct adjective agreement.

## Now try this

Write 200 words about where you:
- usually stay on holiday
- once stayed on holiday
- will stay next holiday
- would like to stay.

# Staying in a hotel

Be prepared to talk about where you stay on holiday – and don't forget negatives!

## Loger dans un hôtel

| | |
|---|---|
| ascenseur (m) | lift |
| escalier (m) | staircase |
| avec douche / bain | with shower / bath |
| salle de bains (f) | bathroom |
| clef / clé (f) | key |
| premier / deuxième étage (m) | first / second floor |
| rez-de-chaussée (m) | ground floor |
| liste des prix (f) / tarif (m) | price list |
| réception (f) | reception |
| parking (m) | car park |
| porte d'entrée (f) | entrance |
| jardin (m) | garden |
| salle de jeux (f) | games room |
| climatisation (f) | air conditioning |
| donner sur la plage | to look on to the beach |
| fonctionner / marcher | to work |

### Negatives
> Page 101

Ne / n' (before a vowel) comes before the verb

ne + pas = not

ne + plus = no longer

ne + jamais = never

ne + personne = nobody

ne + guère = hardly

ne + que = only

ne + rien = nothing

ne + ni + ni = neither ... nor ...

La climatisation ne marchait pas.
The air conditioning wasn't working.

## Worked example

READING   target A

Read the text and answer the question below **in English**.

Après avoir lu toutes les brochures des hôtels dans le Midi, Lila a choisi un petit hôtel familial qui donnait sur la plage. Il y avait une piscine et une salle de jeux pour les enfants et pour les grands-parents il y avait la climatisation et un ascenseur. Mais, en arrivant toute la famille a été vraiment déçue. L'hôtel était en construction et la famille ne pouvait ni voir la plage ni dormir la nuit à cause du bruit. Il n'y avait rien à faire pour les enfants et la climatisation ne marchait pas. La famille ne retournera jamais à cet hôtel.

- brochures = a cognate meaning 'brochure', but **après avoir lu** (after having read) is more complicated – and if you don't recognise **lu** as the past participle of **lire** (to read), this will set you back from the start.

How did Lila choose her holiday accommodation?
She read all the brochures

- Make sure you answer in English. If you answer in French, it will not be counted.

## Now try this

READING   target A

Answer the questions **in English**.

1  Where did Lila go on holiday?
2  Name one facility for the young and one for older people which made the hotel suitable.
3  Why did the hotel not match the family's expectations? (2)
4  What did the family feel about their stay by the end?

# Camping

If you are giving a presentation, you MUST be prepared for some interaction afterwards. The easiest way to do this is to ask a question of your own.

## Au camping

| | |
|---|---|
| camper | to camp |
| faire du camping | to go camping |
| aire de jeux (f) | play area |
| bloc sanitaire (m) | shower block |
| randonnée (f) | hike |
| lieu (m) | place |
| parc d'attractions (m) | amusement park |
| camping (m) | campsite |
| caravane (f) | caravan |
| emplacement (m) | pitch |
| sac de couchage (m) | sleeping bag |
| eau potable (f) | drinking water |
| en plein air | outside |
| location de vélos (f) | bike hire |
| colonie de vacances (f) | summer camp |

## Alternatives for aller

Try to vary not only the tenses of verbs, but also the verbs themselves.

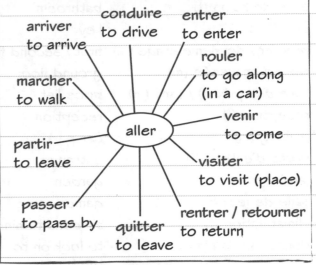

arriver — to arrive
conduire — to drive
entrer — to enter
rouler — to go along (in a car)
marcher — to walk
venir — to come
partir — to leave
aller
visiter — to visit (place)
passer — to pass by
quitter — to leave
rentrer / retourner — to return

## Worked example  🔊 SPEAKING

Parle de tes vacances.

Chaque année je retourne au même camping avec ma famille. Le voyage dure trois heures en voiture et le camping se trouve au bord du lac. J'aime bien faire des excursions au parc d'attractions et à la mer, mais ce que je n'aime pas, ce sont les randonnées fatigantes en haute montagne.

**AIMING HIGHER** Les grandes vacances, c'est le meilleur moment de l'année parce que je quitte la maison pour aller en colonie de vacances. J'adore ça et cet été on va camper en plein air! J'attends mes vacances avec beaucoup d'impatience parce que ça sera une nouvelle expérience pour moi. J'espère qu'il fera beau et qu'il ne pleuvra pas tout le temps!

**CONTROLLED ASSESSMENT**

Presentations should last for at least ONE minute. Shorter presentations will not help you aim for a higher grade.

Remember to think of some questions of your own which you can ask.

This student has restricted herself to the present tense, but she has given a positive **and** a negative opinion of her stay.

Here, the student is talking about a specific camping trip in the **future**.

The use of expressions such as **J'espère que** (I hope that) confirms the student's ability to use more complex language.

## Now try this  🔊 SPEAKING

Choose a photo (or picture from a magazine) of a campsite and answer these questions on it.

- C'est où ce camping?
- Combien de temps avez-vous passé là-bas?
- Qu'est-ce que vous avez fait?
- C'était bien?
- Le camping, c'est comment, à votre avis?

# Holiday preferences

This page will help you give opinions in lots of different ways.

## Les vacances que j'aime

| | |
|---|---|
| C'est / C'était … | It is / was … |
| chouette / génial | great |
| fantastique / formidable | brilliant |
| intéressant / ennuyeux | interesting / boring |

Ce que j'aime, / What I like is
c'est me faire bronzer. / sunbathing.

Ce n'est pas mon truc. / It's not my thing.

Le plus important, / The most important
c'est de faire du sport. / thing is to do sport.

Quand j'étais petit(e), / When I was young
ça allait. / it was OK.

J'adore être en plein / I love being outdoors,
air, même quand il pleut. / even when it rains.

Ce que j'aime le plus, / What I like the most,
c'est aller à la piscine. / is going to the pool.

### Expressing likes and dislikes

| | |
|---|---|
| adorer | to love |
| aimer | to like |
| préférer | to prefer — + infinitive |
| je n'aime pas | I dislike |
| détester | to hate |

J'adore faire du camping.
I love camping.

Je préfère aller
à la campagne.

## Worked example

WRITING

Write about holidays you don't like!

L'été dernier je suis allée à Londres, mais je n'ai pas du tout aimé. Je déteste visiter des monuments et des sites historiques, parce que ce n'est pas mon truc. Ce que j'aime faire, c'est aller à la piscine et me faire bronzer toute la journée avec mes copains.

**AIMING HIGHER**

D'habitude nous restons dans un grand gîte au bord de la mer, mais cette année on va passer des vacances à la campagne parce qu'il faut économiser. Nous allons faire du camping et ce n'est pas mon truc! Mon père a trouvé un petit camping pas cher dans une forêt, mais je préférerais aller à la plage parce que j'adore nager et me faire bronzer.

## CONTROLLED ASSESSMENT

To aim for a higher grade, you must link your sentences into a coherent whole. Even linking sentences with a simple conjunction such as **mais** (but) will help your work to flow.

This answer starts off with recounting a **past** holiday + opinion in the **past**, and then switches to the present tense and expresses a preference.

- This version uses lots of tenses: present, past, future, conditional.
- Different parts of the verbs are used.
- Correct adjective agreements and interesting vocabulary are indicators of a top level student.

## Now try this

WRITING

Write 100 words about your holiday preferences. Include information about what:

- you usually do
- you are doing this year
- your opinion is.

Read through your text carefully – does it hang together well?

# Holiday activities

Be prepared to talk about what you did on holiday, as well as about where you went.

## Activités de vacances

On peut ...    You can ...

faire de l'escalade    faire du patin à glace    se détendre

faire du vélo    faire de la natation    faire de la voile

faire du ski    faire une promenade    jouer au tennis

### How to say 'this' and 'these'

Page 84

| | |
|---|---|
| ce | this + masculine nouns |
| cet | this + any masculine noun starting with a vowel or silent h |
| cette | this + feminine nouns |
| ces | these + ALL plural nouns |

Cet été je vais en France.
I am going to France this summer.

Cette visite guidée est chère.
This guided visit is expensive.

Ces jeunes ont pris des cours de tennis.
These youngsters did a tennis course.

---

## Worked example

READING    target D

Read about the holiday events on offer and answer the question below.

La municipalité a décidé d'organiser tout un programme d'activités pour les jeunes de tout âge cet été. Il y a des visites guidées de la vieille ville et une grande variété d'activités sportives au stade municipal. En cas de mauvais temps, et pour ceux qui préfèrent rester à l'intérieur, il y a la possibilité d'essayer une nouvelle langue ou d'apprendre à faire de la cuisine italienne ou chinoise à la maison des jeunes. Chaque après-midi au musée, il y a des cours sur l'histoire et la vie culturelle de la région. Au théâtre Racine, les petits peuvent regarder des dessins animés tous les jours à 11 heures.

Correct or not?
The town has organised a range of activities. ✓

Most of the statements below refer to material in the text, but only four of them are accurate. You have to be able to appreciate ideas rather than just have a simple knowledge of vocabulary.

A  The events are taking place in December.
B  There are no outdoor events.
C  You can learn a new language.
D  You can learn to cook French specialities.
E  There are activities for very young children.
F  You can learn about history in the afternoon.
G  There are lots of sporting activities available.
H  If you want to see films, you should go to the youth club.

---

## Now try this

READING    target D

Which four statements from A–H above are correct?

# Booking accommodation

Make sure you learn this vocabulary, as it may well crop up in a listening exam.

## Réserver le logement

| | |
|---|---|
| balcon (m) | balcony |
| chambre (pour une personne) (f) | single room |
| chambre pour deux personnes (f) | double room |
| chambre double (f) | double room |
| pour trois nuits | for three nights |
| vue (f) | view |
| bon séjour | have a nice stay |
| hôtesse d'accueil / réceptionniste (f) | receptionist |
| accueil (m) | welcome |
| bagages (mpl) | luggage |
| demi-pension (f) | half-board |
| pension-complète (f) | full board |
| compris / inclus | included |
| Nous allons arriver vers minuit. | We are going to arrive around midnight. |

### Using pouvoir
Page 93

**PRESENT**

| | |
|---|---|
| je peux | I can |
| tu peux | you can |
| il / elle / on peut | he / she / one can |
| nous pouvons | we can |
| vous pouvez | you can |
| ils / elles peuvent | they can |

**IMPERFECT**
je pouvais = I used to be able to

**FUTURE**
je pourrai = I will be able to

**CONDITIONAL** je pourrais = I could

Nous pouvons nager dans la mer. We can swim in the sea

## Worked example
LISTENING 18  target C

Mrs Carpenter is confirming her hotel reservation. Put a cross in the correct box.

Mrs Carpenter is ringing because …

A she wants to book a single room. ☐

B there will be one fewer person in her group. ☒

C she wants to change the date she will arrive. ☐

### EXAM ALERT!

Failure to recognise the negative in sentences led to many incorrect answers to this exam question. Many students incorrectly ticked answer A, as they missed the **ne peut pas venir** (can't come) and **nous n'avons pas besoin de** (we don't need) phrases.

This was a real exam question that a lot of students struggled with – **be prepared!**  ResultsPlus

– Allô. Hôtel Bon Séjour, je vous écoute.

– J'ai une réservation pour trois chambres pour ce weekend au nom de Carpenter. Mon fils ne peut pas venir donc nous n'avons pas besoin de la chambre pour une personne.

- Single words such as **avant** (before), **vers** (towards / around) and **nouvelle** (new) can be crucial to understanding dialogues.
- You can use a process of elimination in questions like these, but make sure you have not eliminated the **correct** answer when you listen to the extract for the second time.

## Now try this
LISTENING 19  target C

Listen to the rest of the recording. Put a cross in the correct boxes.

1 Mrs Carpenter's rooms …
  A have a balcony. ☐
  B look on to the sea. ☐
  C look on to a park. ☐

2 The Carpenter family will be arriving …
  A in the early morning. ☐
  B in the early evening. ☐
  C late at night. ☐

# Holiday plans

Make sure you know the future tense in order to talk about holiday plans. Ring the changes by using the nous form as well as the je form.

## Projets de vacances

| | |
|---|---|
| pendant les grandes vacances | in the summer holiday(s) |
| les vacances de neige | winter sports holiday |
| l'été (m) / l'hiver (m) prochain | next summer / winter |
| demain | tomorrow |
| après-demain | the day after tomorrow |
| le lendemain | the next day |
| louer | to rent |
| passer la journée | to spend the day |
| port de pêche (m) | fishing port |
| court de tennis (m) | tennis court |
| terrain de golf (m) | golf course |

## The nous form in the future

NEAR FUTURE

Nous allons voyager en Afrique.
We are going to travel across Africa.

FUTURE TENSE

Nous irons en Autriche.
We will be going to Austria.

Nous aurons une chambre dans un hôtel.
We will have a room in a hotel.

Nous ferons de la planche à voile.
We will do windsurfing.

## Worked example

**WRITING**

Write about your holiday plans for this year.

Pendant les grandes vacances j'irai au Lavandou avec ma famille. Nous louerons un appartement dans une grande résidence avec piscine à cinq cent mètres de la plage. On y va depuis huit ans!

**AIMING HIGHER**

Voulez-vous passer des vacances avec moi? L'été prochain nous irons dans une station balnéaire où il y a l'une des plus belles plages d'Europe. Vous y trouverez cinquante plages, six ports de pêche et de plaisance et plus de cent courts de tennis. Vous pourriez jouer au golf sur un des deux terrains de golf à 18 et 9 trous.

## Aiming higher

In your writing tasks, remember to use different tenses, descriptions and opinions as well as more complex language, in order to achieve the best written work.

**1** For added VARIETY, swap between the nous form nous allons and the on form on va (same ending as third person singular).

**2** Add a RHETORICAL QUESTION to the reader, such as Voulez-vous passer des vacances avec moi?

**3** Include DIFFERENT STRUCTURES in your writing, such as depuis + present tense, as well as the future tense with nous and je.

## Now try this

Write 150 words about your future holiday plans.

Make sure you include:
- several forms of verbs (vous, je, nous, on)
- several tenses (future, present)
- comparative and superlative
- interesting vocabulary.

# Holiday experiences

'Past holidays' is a popular topic for reading exams. Make sure you learn winter holiday vocabulary too, as France is a big skiing country.

## Souvenirs de vacances

| | |
|---|---|
| en hiver | in winter |
| vacances d'hiver (fpl) | winter holidays |
| stage de ski (m) | skiing course |
| l'hébergement (m) | accommodation |
| société (f) | company |
| nourriture (f) | food |
| suffisant(e) | sufficient / enough |
| j'ai fait | I did |
| c'était | it was |
| les vacances étaient … | the holidays were … |
| on avait faim | we were hungry |
| nous sommes sortis | we went out |
| nous avons choisi | we chose |
| nous avons partagé | we shared |

J'ai fait du snowboard.

## Perfect tense: être verbs » Page 96

Je suis

- allé(e)(s) — went
- arrivé(e)(s) — arrived
- entré(e)(s) — entered
- monté(e)(s) — went up
- rentré(e)(s) / retourné(e) — returned
- tombé(e)(s) — fell
- venu(e)(s) — came
- descendu(e)(s) — went down
- parti(e)(s) — left
- sorti(e)(s) — went out

The past participle has to AGREE with the subject:

je suis allé = I went (one male)

elle est allée = she went

vous êtes allés = you went (2+ males)

---

## Worked example   READING   target B

Read the text and answer the question in English about Baptiste's holiday.

> L'année dernière, en hiver, j'ai fait un stage de ski UCPA avec mon meilleur copain Brice. L'UCPA est une société qui organise des vacances sportives.
> Nous avons choisi un stage de ski à La Plagne dans les Alpes. C'était un stage pour les ados de 13 à 17 ans. L'hébergement était dans un chalet énorme. Nous avons partagé notre chambre avec deux autres garçons qui faisaient le même stage.
> La nourriture était suffisante mais nous sommes souvent sortis le soir pour aller à la pizzeria parce qu'on avait une faim de loup après la journée sur les pistes.

When was the holiday exactly?    last winter

## Reading carefully

- First, read the text through quickly to get an idea of what it's about.
- Read the text again and make sure you understand the tenses, etc.
- Read the questions carefully and be precise in how you answer them.

- Read the question **carefully** – here you are asked when **exactly** Baptiste went on holiday – you will need to write last + winter to score.

---

## Now try this   READING   target B

Answer these questions on the text above.
1 Who did Baptiste go on holiday with?
2 Were there any restrictions to the holiday?
3 Give two details about the accommodation.
4 Why did they often go out to eat?

Be precise in your answer here – what **sort** of friend is Brice exactly?

Don't say **where**, say **why**.

# Directions

Look at this vocabulary and then see if you can direct somebody from your house to the shops.

## Les directions

**Tournez à gauche.**
Turn left.

**Tournez à droite.**
Turn right.

**Allez tout droit.**
Go straight on.

**Au coin, tournez à droite.**
Turn right at the corner.

**Traversez le pont.**
Cross the bridge.

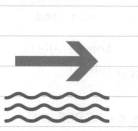

**Traversez la rivière.**
Cross the river.

**Allez tout droit aux feux.**
Go straight on at the lights.

**Allez jusqu'au carrefour.**
Go to the crossroads.

**Prenez la deuxiéme rue à droite.**
Take the second road on the right.

**Prenez la première rue à gauche.**
Take the first road on the left.

> Don't confuse **tout droit** (straight on) with **à droite** (on the right).

## Worked example

LISTENING 20   target D

Listen and choose the correct direction.

A left, then right, then over the lights ☐
B second right, straight on, left at lights ☒
C second right, right at the lights, station on the left ☐

– Pour aller à la gare, vous prenez la deuxième rue à droite … puis allez tout droit jusqu'aux feux, tournez à gauche et la gare est située sur votre droite.

## Learning vocabulary

How do you learn vocabulary? You can:

- make yourself LEARNING CARDS – French on one side, English on the other, or a picture on one side and French on the other.
- use learning cards to help you learn your assessments. Write KEY WORDS on them as well as phrases in different tenses which you find particularly tricky.

Traversez le pont.

## Now try this

WRITING

Write instructions in 50 words for the other two sets of directions above.

# Public transport

Use this vocabulary to say how you get to school and how you go on holiday.

## Le transport

en auto / voiture     en train     en bateau     en métro     en autobus (arrêt d'autobus = bus stop)

en car     en / à bicyclette / vélo     en avion     en camion     à pied

## Worked example

READING · target C

Read the text and circle the correct answer below.

> L'année dernière pendant les grandes vacances nous sommes allés en Angleterre. Nous sommes partis de chez nous en voiture. Nous avons pris le tunnel sous la Manche en train, on met la voiture dans le train. Comme mon père n'aimait pas conduire à gauche nous avons loué des vélos pour nous balader et nous avons utilisé les transports en commun pour aller en ville.

The journey began by (car) / train / boat.

### Different uses of en

en voiture = by car

en hiver = in winter

en ville = to town

transports en commun = public transport

Lots of transport is mentioned in this short text, but it is the one which **began** the journey that you need to identify – *partis de chez nous* (left home) is a big clue to help you.

## Now try this

READING · target C

Read the text above again. Circle the correct answers.

(a) They crossed **France / the Channel / Europe** by train.

(b) Once in England they used their car **a lot / a little / to give people lifts**.

(c) They hired **bikes / a boat / a coach** to get around.

(d) They went into town **on the bus / by car / on foot**.

Be careful with this one – you have to deduce!

39

# Transport

As well as revising the vocabulary on this page, make sure you know your numbers. They can be useful in this topic.

Le vol a un retard de deux heures.

## Le transport

| | |
|---|---|
| aéroport (m) | airport |
| vol (m) | flight |
| voyage (m) | journey |
| autoroute (f) | motorway |
| déviation (f) | detour / diversion |
| essence (f) | petrol |
| heures de pointe (fpl) | rush hour |
| panne (f) | breakdown |
| péage (m) | toll |
| poids lourds (m) | heavy goods vehicle |
| priorité à droite | priority to the right |
| route (f) | road |
| trajet (m) | route, trip |
| sens interdit / unique (m) | one-way system |
| retard (m) | delay |

## avoir and être

> Page 91

TWO KEY verbs which need to be learnt!

| ÊTRE | TO BE |
|---|---|
| je suis | I am |
| tu es | you are |
| il / elle / on est | he / she / one is |
| nous sommes | we are |
| vous êtes | you are |
| ils / elles sont | they are |

| AVOIR | TO HAVE |
|---|---|
| j'ai | I have |
| tu as | you have |
| il / elle / on a | he / she / one has |
| nous avons | we have |
| vous avez | you have |
| ils / elles ont | they have |

## Worked example

🎧 21  target A

You hear this announcement about a flight delay. Note the details in English.

**(a)** Country of destination

Switzerland

**(b)** Flight number: AF? 250

**(c)** The new departure time 15.30

**(d)** Reason for the delay Snowfall

– Le vol à destination de Genève en Suisse, vol AF 250, a un retard de deux heures. L'avion va partir à 15h30. Nous nous excusons de ce retard qui est dû aux chutes de neige.

chutes de neige = snowfall
Don't be misled by hearing 'false friends'. Here, chutes have nothing to do with 'shoot' but if you hear neige (snow) you will have the correct answer (snowfall / heavy snow).

## EXAM ALERT!

Surprisingly, there were some students who answered this question in French and, therefore, were not awarded marks. Common incorrect answers were Sweden, Spain and USA.

This was a real exam question that a lot of students struggled with – **be prepared!**

ResultsPlus

- Listen for numbers really carefully – the questions warn you that there are numbers to listen for, so be prepared.

- Remember, cent = 100 so deux-cents = 200. Then you need to add the next number cinquante (50), so the answer is 250.

- With times, listen first for the hour. Write that down, then listen to the minutes which come next, here trente (30).

## Now try this

🎧 22  target A

Listen to the report and note the details in English.

**(a)** Country of destination

**(b)** Motorway number: A?

**(c)** When the road will open

**(d)** Reason for the closure

# At the café

You may already know lots of food vocabulary, but watch out for false friends, for example, les chips = crisps!

## Au café

| | |
|---|---|
| baguette (f) | French stick |
| brochette (f) | kebab |
| côtelette (f) | chop |
| frites (fpl) | chips |
| hamburger (m) | hamburger |
| moutarde (f) | mustard |
| omelette (f) | omelette |
| pizza (f) | pizza |
| poisson (m) | fish |
| poulet (m) | chicken |
| riz (m) | rice |
| rôti (m) | roast |
| salade verte (f) | green salad |
| saucisse (f) | sausage |
| soupe (f) | soup |
| tartine (f) | slice of bread and butter |
| viande (f) | meat |

## Using the verb vouloir

Page 93

**PRESENT**

| | | | |
|---|---|---|---|
| je veux | I want | nous voulons | we want |
| tu veux | you want | vous voulez | you want |
| il / elle veut | he / she wants | ils / elles veulent | they want |

Je veux manger. I want to eat.

Nous voulons aller au restaurant.
We want to go to a restaurant.

Elle veut commander
un sandwich.
She wants to order
a sandwich.

**PERFECT** j'ai voulu = I wanted

**IMPERFECT** je voulais = I used to want

**FUTURE** je voudrai = I will want

**CONDITIONAL** je voudrais = I would like

---

## Worked example

LISTENING 23 — target G

Listen. What does this person want to eat? B

A B
C D
E F

– Je voudrais une pizza.

### EXAM ALERT!

This vocabulary was generally well known. However, students sometimes made silly mistakes, so make sure you look carefully at the pictures and think of the French words before you listen.

This was a real exam question that a lot of students struggled with – **be prepared!**

ResultsPlus

---

## Now try this

LISTENING 24 — target G

Now, complete the activity above for these four people by putting a cross in the correct boxes.

| | A | B | C | D | E | F |
|---|---|---|---|---|---|---|
| 1 | | | | | | |
| 2 | | | | | | |
| 3 | | | | | | |
| 4 | | | | | | |

# Eating in a café

Make sure you revise plenty of food words – they are very likely to feature somewhere!

## Manger au café

| | |
|---|---|
| beurre (m) | butter |
| bifteck (m) | steak |
| confiture (f) | jam |
| crêpe (f) | pancake |
| croissant (m) | croissant |
| croque-monsieur (m) | cheese and ham toastie |
| gâteau (m) | cake |
| miel (m) | honey |
| pain (m) | bread |
| pâtes (fpl) | pasta |
| café (m) | coffee |
| chocolat chaud (m) | hot chocolate |
| eau minérale (f) | mineral water |
| jus de fruit (m) | fruit juice |
| lait (m) | milk |
| limonade / Orangina (f) | lemonade / Orangina |
| thé (m) | tea |

## Talking about food flavours

In French you can't just say 'a milky coffee' or 'a ham sandwich'; you have to use a form of à.

un café au lait          a milky coffee

| masculine | feminine | plural |
|---|---|---|
| au<br>à l' after vowel or silent h | à la<br>à l' after vowel or silent h | aux |

un café au lait

une glace à la fraise

des crêpes aux pommes

une tarte à l'abricot

## Worked example

LISTENING 25 | target E

Listen. What does Mélissa order?

A Hot chocolate, croissant and jam ☐
B Iced chocolate and croissant ☐
C Hot chocolate and croissant ☒

– Qu'est-ce que vous désirez?
– Euh … Je veux un chocolat chaud.
– Et avec ça?
– Un croissant.
– Avec beurre et confiture?
– Non, merci.

## Listening strategies

- People sometimes CHANGE THEIR MINDS, so don't assume they are ordering every item of food you hear mentioned.

- Make sure you listen to the WHOLE DIALOGUE and check what the person actually orders. It might not be what they originally wanted, or they might be offered something else which they don't want.

- Listen for phrases such as je regrette (I'm sorry) which might tell you that something is not available, or non, merci which tells you they do not want what is on offer.

## Now try this

LISTENING 26 | target E

Listen. What do Olivier and Adèle order? Put a cross in the correct box.

**Olivier**

A Black coffee, croissant with jam ☐
B White coffee, croissant with honey ☐
C White coffee, croissant with butter ☐

**Adèle**

A Mineral water and pancake ☐
B Toasted sandwich and mineral water ☐
C Toasted sandwich and fruit juice ☐

# Eating in a restaurant

You might need to understand opinions on restaurants as well as what you eat in them!

## Manger au restaurant

| | |
|---|---|
| assiette (f) | plate |
| couteau (m) | knife |
| cuillère (f) | spoon |
| fourchette (f) | fork |
| verre (m) | glass |
| nappe (f) | tablecloth |
| serviette (f) | napkin |
| hors d'oeuvre (m) | starter |
| plat principal (m) | main course |
| dessert (m) | dessert |
| boisson (f) | drink |
| menu (m) / carte (f) | menu |
| menu (à prix fixe) (m) | fixed price menu |
| plat (du jour) (m) | dish (of the day) |
| plats à emporter (mpl) | takeaway |
| pourboire (m) | tip |
| service (non) compris | service (not) included |
| self-service / self (m) | self-service restaurant |
| snack (m) | snack bar |

### Saying 'there'
≫ Page 87

Use **y** to say 'there' in French and to replace **à** + noun after a verb.

| | |
|---|---|
| Je vais au café. | I'm going to the café. |
| ➡ j'y vais. | I'm going there. |
| Je joue au football. | I play football. |
| ➡ j'y joue. | I play it (football). |

**IDIOMS WITH Y**

| | |
|---|---|
| Il y a deux cafés. | There are two cafés. |
| Il y a trois jours. | Three days ago. |
| On y va! | Let's go! |
| Allons-y! | Let's go! |
| Ça y est. | That's it! |

Nous y allons pour des fêtes.
We go there for parties.

---

## Worked example 🎧 27 / target D

Listen. Who says the following: Léna, Malik or Laetitia?
I love going to restaurants.   Léna

– Écoutons d'abord Léna.
– J'adore aller au restaurant mais c'est cher. Nous y allons seulement pour des fêtes, les anniversaires par exemple.

### EXAM ALERT!

This task asks students to discriminate between answers, based on likes and dislikes.

- Listen carefully for the names before each speaker in listening tasks like this.
- Don't jump to conclusions as soon as you hear a key word, but wait and see if there is an opinion accompanying it.

This was a real exam question that a lot of students struggled with – **be prepared!**  ResultsPlus

---

## Now try this 🎧 28 / target D

Listen to the whole recording. Who says the following? Put a cross in the correct boxes.

|  | Léna | Malik | Laetitia |
|---|---|---|---|
| **(a)** I like small restaurants. | ☐ | ☐ | ☐ |
| **(b)** I only go on special occasions. | ☐ | ☐ | ☐ |
| **(c)** I like self-service restaurants. | ☐ | ☐ | ☐ |
| **(d)** I go out to a restaurant every week. | ☐ | ☐ | ☐ |

You need to listen to the **whole passage** in this sort of listening task, as sometimes the answers are not what you think – here you will hear one speaker say they **déteste** (hate) self-service restaurants and another say they **préfère les self-services**.

# Opinions about food

Make sure you can say what food you really like – and what you hate!

## Ce que j'aime manger

| | |
|---|---|
| J'adore l'ail. | I love garlic. |
| Je déteste les spaghettis. | I hate spaghetti. |
| Je trouve les pizzas malsaines. | I think pizzas are unhealthy. |
| malade | ill |
| bien cuit(e) | well cooked, well done |
| escargots (mpl) | snails |
| plein de goût | tasty |
| amer / amère | bitter |
| goûteux/euse | tasty |
| dégoûtant(e) | disgusting |
| délicieux/euse | delicious |
| (trop) épicé(e) | (too) spicy |
| salé(e) | salty |
| sucré(e) | sweet |

## Time adverbs

Add time expressions wherever you can.

| | |
|---|---|
| chaque jour | every day |
| quelquefois | sometimes |
| de temps en temps | now and again |
| souvent | often |
| toujours | always |
| ne ... jamais | never |
| rarement | seldom |
| une fois par semaine | once a week |

Je mange toujours des repas légers.
I always eat low-fat meals.
Quelquefois je mangeais au Quick.
I sometimes used to eat at the snack bar.

Je ne mangerai jamais d'escargots.
I will never eat snails.

## Worked example

**WRITING**

Write about your food preferences.

> Je ne mange jamais de spaghettis parce que je n'aime pas le goût. Je préfère manger du poulet-frites et j'en mange souvent à la cantine. À la cantine, les frites sont super bonnes.

This answer keeps to the present but uses some good vocabulary.

**AIMING HIGHER**

> Moi, je ne mange pas souvent de curry, parce que je trouve ça trop épicé et l'année dernière j'ai été malade après une soirée au resto indien. La semaine prochaine, je vais aller au restaurant mexicain avec ma copine pour manger du biftek bien cuit, parce que nous adorons ça, tous les deux. Mais le plat que j'adore le plus, ce sont les escargots (ma copine les déteste!). Mon repas idéal serait un plat d'escargots avec du beurre et de l'ail.

## Aiming higher

1 Use NEGATIVES in your written work to show you know how to use them.

2 If you are giving an opinion about food, try to JUSTIFY it by saying why you have that opinion.

3 Working a variety of TENSES into your writing is not always easy, but try and include as much variety as you can.

This answer includes present (eating habits), past (an eating experience), future (plans for a birthday meal) and conditional (ideal meal). It also uses longer sentences joining clauses with **et**, **mais** and **parce que**.

## Now try this

**WRITING**

Write 60 to 100 words giving your own opinions on food – try to use more than two tenses.

# Restaurant review

Use this page to help you deal with problems at a restaurant.

## Se plaindre au restaurant

| | |
|---|---|
| bouteille (f) | bottle |
| steak-frites (m) | steak and chips |
| vin rouge / blanc (m) | red / white wine |
| réserver une table | to reserve a table |
| choisir | to choose |
| commander | to order |
| demander l'addition | to ask for the bill |
| dîner | to have dinner |
| revenir | to return |
| serveur / serveuse | waiter / waitress |
| cher / chère | expensive |
| froid / chaud | cold / hot |

C'était trop sucré / salé.
It was too sweet / salty

La viande n'était pas bien cuite.
The meat wasn't well cooked.

### Using the verb devoir
Page 93

| | |
|---|---|
| je dois | I have to |
| tu dois | you have to |
| il / elle / on doit | he / she / one has to |
| nous devons | we have to |
| vous devez | you have to |
| ils / elles doivent | they have to |

PERFECT j'ai dû = I had to

IMPERFECT je devais = I had to / used to have to

FUTURE je devrai = I will have to

CONDITIONAL je devrais = I would have to

Je ne dois pas manger trop de gâteau.
I shouldn't eat too much cake.

## Worked example — READING — target C

Read this extract from a letter of complaint.

*Nous avons réservé une table pour 20 heures, mais nous avons dû attendre une demi-heure dans le bar. Ma femme a choisi le steak-frites, mais tout était froid. On a commandé une bouteille de vin rouge, mais le serveur nous a apporté du vin blanc. On a voulu manger un dessert, mais le serveur n'est pas revenu à notre table et, après une demi-heure, j'ai demandé l'addition. Heureusement, ce n'était pas cher. Quand la fille est allée chercher nos manteaux, elle n'a pas pu trouver mon chapeau, mais on a dû partir, parce que ma femme était malade ...*
M. Autrete

## EXAM ALERT!

Some students jumped to the wrong conclusion as they spotted 20 in the letter and twenty as an answer. They thought they go together perfectly – they do NOT!

This was a real exam question that a lot of students struggled with – **be prepared!**

ResultsPlus

Put a cross in the correct box.

The family went to their table

(i) twenty minutes late ☐

(ii) thirty minutes late ☒

(iii) an hour late ☐

The bit you need to read for this first question is **Nous avons dû attendre une demi-heure** (We had to wait half an hour). If you were familiar with the past tense of **devoir** (see above), you would have found this easily.

## Now try this — READING — target C

Many students found (c) particularly challenging, so read the letter carefully.

Underline the correct answer.

(a) The main course was **undercooked / cold / not what was ordered**.

(b) The waiter made a mistake with the **dessert / wine / bill**.

(c) At the end of the evening **they were overcharged / M. Autrete was ill / something was lost**.

# Shops

Make sure you learn the names of shops. Notice that all those ending in 'ie' are feminine.

## Des magasins

| | |
|---|---|
| bijouterie (f) | jeweller's |
| boucherie (f) | butcher's |
| charcuterie (f) | delicatessen |
| chocolaterie (f) | chocolate shop |
| confiserie (f) | sweet shop |
| fleuriste (m) | florist's |
| hypermarché (m) | hypermarket |
| librairie (f) | bookshop |
| pâtisserie (f) | cake shop |
| pharmacie (f) | chemist's |
| poissonnerie (f) | fishmonger's |
| supermarché (m) | supermarket |
| tabac (m) | tobacconist's |

## Present tense of -er verbs

Page 89

Use the present tense to talk about what you are doing NOW or do REGULARLY.

| JOUER | TO PLAY |
|---|---|
| je joue | I play |
| tu joues | you play |
| il / elle / on joue | he / she / one plays |
| nous jouons | we play |
| vous jouez | you play |
| ils / elles jouent | they play |
| Aimes-tu ce magasin? | Do you like this shop? |
| Nous achetons du poisson. | We buy / are buying fish. |

Notice how the je, tu, il / elle and ils / elles forms can change!

acheter — to buy ➡ j'achète — I buy

préférer — to prefer ➡ elle préfère — she prefers

## Worked example

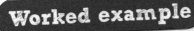
**READING** **target G**

Read the sign on this shop.

What does this shop sell?   perfume

Read the sign carefully – it is the sort of cognate you should easily recognise in reading and listening passages.

## Learning vocabulary

In the reading and listening exams you are going to have to recognise French words, not produce them, so when you are learning vocabulary, concentrate on testing yourself on French to English, rather than the other way round.

## Now try this

**READING** **target G**

What do these shops sell? Link them to their English meanings.

1  un magasin de sport
2  un magasin de bricolage
3  un magasin de meubles
4  un magasin de musique
5  un magasin de jouets

a  toy shop
b  music shop
c  DIY shop
d  furniture shop
e  sports shop
f  clothes shop

jouer = to play, so you should be able to work out what jouets means.

# Shopping for food

Quantities are useful expressions to know when shopping in France!

## Faire les courses

| | |
|---|---|
| un kilo de | a kilo of |
| un litre de | a litre of |
| un morceau de | a piece of |
| un paquet de | a packet of |
| un peu de | a little of/a few |
| un pot de | a jar of |
| un tiers de | a third of |
| une boîte de | a box of |
| une bouteille de | a bottle of |
| une douzaine de | a dozen |
| une tranche de | a slice of |
| champignon (m) | mushroom |
| chou (m) | cabbage |
| fraise / pomme (f) | strawberry / apple |
| œuf (m) | egg |
| pain au chocolat (m) | chocolate pastry |
| pêche (f) | peach |
| pomme de terre (f) | potato |
| yaourt (m) | yoghurt |

## Quantities

After quantities de does not change to agree with the noun. It stays as de. Before a vowel, it becomes d'.

| | |
|---|---|
| assez de | enough |
| beaucoup de | lots of |
| encore de | more |
| moins de | less |
| pas mal de | quite a few |
| plein de | a lot of |
| plus de | more |

Elle a assez de bananes.
She's got enough bananas.

Tu as trop d'argent.
You have got too much money.

Il y a plein de pommes.
There are plenty of apples.

## Worked example 🎧29 target F-E

Listen to the students and answer the question **in English**.

How much milk is needed?   two litres

– Nous avons besoin d'un litre de lait.
– Un litre de l…
– Non, pardon, j'ai voulu dire deux litres de lait.
– Pas de problème – je vais acheter deux litres de lait.

nous avons besoin de = we need

## More listening strategies

- Don't be too hasty to write down your answers – requests sometimes change, so you need to listen until the end!
- If you do change your mind about an answer, make sure you cross it out completely and write the correct answer clearly instead.
- When speaking normally, especially in dialogues, people often use 'thinking' noises, but don't be put off by them! You can use your own 'thinking' noises to gain time in your speaking assessment.

Euh … Er …        Ah … Er …

Attends / attendez …   Er, wait …

## Now try this 🎧30 target F-E

Listen to the rest of the dialogue. What quantity of these items is needed?

(a) Eggs
(b) Sugar
(c) Chocolate pastries
(d) Strawberry jam
(e) Yoghurts
(f) Mineral water

# Shopping

You need to be able to describe items you would like to buy – remembering to make adjectives agree.

## Faire des achats

| | |
|---|---|
| magasin de vêtements (m) | clothes shop |
| bonnet (m) | hat / beanie |
| bracelet (m) | bracelet |
| casquette (f) | cap |
| ceinture (f) | belt |
| chapeau (m) | hat |
| maquillage (m) | make-up |
| mode (f) | fashion |
| musique (f) | music |
| rouge à lèvres (m) | lipstick |
| sac à dos (m) | rucksack |
| sac à main (m) | handbag |
| vêtements (mpl) | clothes |
| efficace | efficient |
| relier | to link / connect |
| fonctionner | to work |

### Using the adjective 'new'

> Page 81

nouveau (new) = irregular adjective used in front of noun: un nouveau livre (a new book).

| singular | | plural | |
|---|---|---|---|
| masc | fem | masc | fem |
| nouveau | nouvelle | nouveaux | nouvelles |

nouvel (for masculine nouns starting with a vowel or silent h)

| | |
|---|---|
| un nouveau collier | a new necklace |
| un nouvel accessoire | a new accessory |
| une nouvelle bague | a new ring |

When 'new' means 'different', e.g. you want a new glass to replace a dirty one, use autre (other): Est-ce que je peux avoir un autre verre? Can I have another glass?

---

## Worked example

READING | target A

Read the text and answer the question below.

**Le bonnet MP3**

C'est le nouvel accessoire indispensable pour les jeunes, les fanatiques de la mode et de la bonne musique. Vous pouvez tout simplement relier votre lecteur MP3 au récepteur fourni dans votre bonnet. Puis mettez le récepteur dans votre poche ou votre sac et écoutez vos chansons favorites – sans fil. La transmission du récepteur au bonnet est efficace jusqu'à 12 mètres. L'émetteur ainsi que le récepteur fonctionnent chacun avec 2 piles AAA (non incluses).

Name two types of people who might buy this product.

young people and music fans

### Reading strategies

In questions aimed at higher grades there will be some vocabulary you won't have revised. Here are some strategies to help you.

- READ the questions in English to find out more information.
- COGNATES and near cognates will help: indispensable, fanatique, musique, accessoire, but be careful piles = batteries (not piles!).
- CONTEXT – the text is about an MP3 player and earphones, so the chances are un récepteur is some sort of receiver (it isn't crucial to know which sort exactly).

---

## Now try this

READING | target A

Answer the questions in English.

1 What do you have to do to make the device work?
2 Which **two** places are suggested for placing the receiver?
3 How close must the receiver be to the earphones?
4 How many batteries come with the hat?

Watch out – a tricky question!

# Signs in shops

You may come across shop signs in the reading exam, so make sure you are familiar with them.

## Des panneaux aux magasins

| | |
|---|---|
| achats (mpl) | purchases |
| ascenseur (m) | lift |
| cabine d'essayage (f) | changing room |
| chariot (m) | shopping trolley |
| caisse (f) | till |
| entrée (f) | entrance |
| escalator (m) | escalator |
| fermer / fermé | to close / closed |
| ouvrir / ouvert | to open / open |
| journée de repos (f) | rest day |
| offre spéciale (f) | special offer |
| panier (m) | shopping basket |
| rayon (m) | department |
| réduction (f) / réduit(e) | reduction / reduced |
| soldes (mpl) | sale |
| sortie (de secours) (f) | (emergency) exit |
| vitrine (f) | shop window |

### 'my', 'your', 'their'

Page 82

| | masc | fem | plural |
|---|---|---|---|
| my | mon | ma | mes |
| your | ton | ta | tes |
| his / her | son | sa | ses |
| our | notre | notre | nos |
| your | votre | votre | vos |
| their | leur | leur | leurs |

Mon panier est plein.
My basket is full.

C'est ton chariot?
Is it your shopping trolley?

Notre offre spéciale finit demain.
Our special offer finishes tomorrow.

> Nos heures d'ouverture:
> mardi au dimanche 9h00 à 19h00
> Fermé le lundi et les jours fériés

## Worked example

READING | target C

Read the text and put a cross by the correct answer.

> **Vous avez jusqu'au trente-et-un janvier pour avoir vingt pour cent de réduction sur les achats. Nos soldes durent jusqu'à la fin du mois. Nous sommes ouverts tous les dimanches.**

You can buy items that are in the sale
A all year ☐
B this month ☒
C next month ☐

- Don't be put off by **numbers** written out in words in reading passages – make sure you can recognise them as vocabulary items if they come up in **times**, **dates** and **ages**, as on this notice.
- Here, it helps to understand the small words **nos** (our), **ce** (this) and **fin** (end) to get the answer right.

## Now try this

READING | target C

Read the sign on the right and put a cross by the correct answer.

If you have bought 12 items, you should pay at till number …

A 5 ☐
B 1 ☐
C 6 ☐

> Moins de dix articles?
> Passez aux caisses
> numéro un à cinq.

# Clothes and colours

Make sure you can describe what you are wearing – and remember that the colour comes AFTER the item.

## Les vêtements et les couleurs

| | |
|---|---|
| baskets (fpl) | trainers |
| casquette (f) | cap |
| chaussettes (fpl) | socks |
| chaussures (fpl) | shoes |
| chemise (f) | shirt |
| jean (m) | jeans |
| jupe (f) | skirt |
| pantalon (m) | trousers |
| pyjama (m) | pyjamas |
| robe (f) | dress |
| sandales (fpl) | sandals |
| short (m) | shorts |
| slip (m) | underpants/briefs |
| sweat (m) | sweatshirt |
| tricot / pullover (m) | jumper |
| t-shirt (m) | T-shirt |

## Position of adjectives

> Page 81

All colours and most other adjectives come AFTER the noun:
la robe bleue = the blue dress.

- rouge
- gris(e)
- jaune
- noir(e)
- marron
- bleu(e)
- vert(e)
- blanc / blanche
- rose

marron does not change in the feminine or plural: une chemise marron; deux chemises marron.
Nor do rose, lilas or orange.

## Worked example

LISTENING 31 | target F

Listen. Which is the worst item of clothing Simon has? E

A   B   C

D   E   F

– Simon?
– Ma mère m'a acheté un pullover.

## EXAM ALERT!

Surprisingly, students did least well at recognising **pullover**, even though it is a cognate. Knowledge of core vocabulary is vital – recognising words both when written down and pronounced out loud.

This was a real exam question that a lot of students struggled with – **be prepared!**

ResultsPlus

- If there are pictures to choose from, try to go through them before you listen and remind yourself of the French words you might hear for each item.
- Common sense will tell you that picture A, of a dress, is unlikely to belong to a boy, Simon.

## Now try this

LISTENING 32 | target F

Listen to the rest of the dialogues. Which is the worst item of clothing each of these people has?

1 Anaïs        3 Marie-Laure
2 François      4 Samir

# Shopping for clothes

If you are talking about clothes shopping in your speaking assessment, be ready to ask as well as answer questions.

## Faire du shopping

| | |
|---|---|
| blouson (m) | casual jacket |
| bottes (fpl) | boots |
| caleçon (m) | boxer shorts/leggings |
| chemise de nuit (f) | nightdress |
| collant (m) | tights |
| cravate (f) | tie |
| écharpe (f) | scarf |
| gilet (m) | cardigan |
| imper(méable) (m) | raincoat |
| maillot de bain (m) | swimming costume/trunks |
| pantoufles (fpl) | slippers |
| survêtement / jogging (m) | tracksuit |
| marque (f) | brand/make/label |
| taille (f) | size |
| ridicule | ridiculous |

## Asking questions

> Page 102

1. Raise your voice to turn a statement into a question.

   Vous aimez acheter des vêtements?
   Do you like buying clothes?

2. Put Est-ce que at the start of a question.

   Est-ce que vous aimez acheter des vêtements?

3. Swap the subject and verb round and add a hyphen.

   Aimez-vous acheter des vêtements?
   Do you like buying clothes?

   Add a -t- between two vowels: Ton frère, aime-t-il faire du shopping?

## Worked example

🔊 SPEAKING

Tu aimes faire du shopping?

> Je n'aime pas trop acheter des vêtements parce que je trouve cela ennuyeux. J'ai mon propre style et je trouve la mode complètement ridicule. Je préfère acheter des magazines ou des livres.

- Good use of **ne ... trop** (not much) makes a change from just using **ne ... pas**.
- Use of **parce que ...** to justify an opinion improves the level.

**AIMING HIGHER**

> J'aime m'habiller à la mode et chaque weekend je vais en ville pour faire du shopping. De temps en temps on peut trouver des marques à de super prix. La semaine dernière, j'ai acheté un t-shirt dans une liquidation de stock. J'étais très heureuse et ce samedi je voudrais retourner en centre-ville chercher des bottes et un blouson!

- Variety of structures, tenses, interesting vocabulary and opinions all help aim for a higher grade. Note the use of present, past (things bought last week) and conditional (**je voudrais retourner**).

## Now try this

🔊 SPEAKING

Answer these questions.

- C'est important pour vous d'être à la mode?
- Aimez-vous faire du shopping?
- Est-ce que vous achetez souvent des marques? Pourquoi (pas)?

You could prepare questions like these to boost your interaction marks.

# Returning items

This page will prepare you for returning problem items – and help you use pronouns correctly.

## Un échange

| | |
|---|---|
| bouton (m) | button |
| pointure (f) | size (shoes) |
| veste (f) | jacket |
| être remboursé(e) | to be refunded |
| reçu (m) | receipt |
| trou (m) | hole |
| il / elle ne me va pas | it doesn't suit me |
| à la mode | fashionable |
| pas assez large | not big enough |
| trop court(e) | too short |
| démodé(e) | old-fashioned |
| dernier / dernière | last |
| fâché(e) | angry |
| déçu(e) | disappointed |

### Saying 'it' and 'them'

> Page 86

masculine = le    feminine = la    plural = les

Je peux le changer?   Can I change it?

Je peux la changer?   Can I change it?

In the perfect tense, put the pronoun before the part of avoir and make it agree!

J'ai acheté une veste.   I bought a jacket.

Je l'ai achetée = I bought it (veste is feminine, so add e to the past participle)

Je voudrais les essayer.
I'd like to try them.

---

## Worked example

WRITING

Write about problems you have had with clothes you have bought.

> Samedi dernier, j'ai acheté une veste, mais quand je suis rentré(e) à la maison j'ai trouvé qu'il manquait un bouton.

**AIMING HIGHER**

> Le dernier vêtement que j'ai acheté était un blouson en cuir. Je l'ai acheté dans une nouvelle boutique près de chez moi, mais en rentrant à la maison, j'ai découvert qu'il y avait un petit trou dans la poche. J'étais fâchée parce que le blouson coûtait cher et en plus j'avais perdu le reçu alors il était impossible d'être remboursée.

You can weave examples of things which have happened to you into most topics. For example, you might want to include a few sentences like these in a presentation on **shopping** or **clothes**.

- Plenty of tenses are used here. Both adjectival positions and endings show this to be an improved answer.
- Correct use of pronouns: Je l'ai acheté (I bought it) is also typical of a better piece of work.

---

## Now try this

Write about an experience you had when you had to return an item to a shop.

Try to include:

Past tense – hier, l'été dernier, j'ai acheté, c'était, il y avait

Relative pronouns – qui/que, e.g. La veste que j'ai achetée

Details – en laine, cher, un trou

Feelings – fâché, triste, ennuyé (annoyed), e.g. J'étais très ennuyé(e)

# Internet shopping

Internet shopping is becoming more and more popular. You may well come across it in a listening text, or choose to talk about it in your assessment.

## Faire du shopping sur Internet

| | |
|---|---|
| envoyer | to send |
| carte de crédit (f) | credit card |
| choix (m) | choice |
| commande (f) | order |
| fraude (f) | fraud |
| livraison (f) | delivery |
| prix (m) | price |
| problème (m) | problem |
| risque (m) | risk |
| société (f) | company |
| connu(e) | known |
| fiable | reliable |
| gratuit(e) | free of charge |
| réduit(e) | reduced |
| de plus en plus | more and more |
| donc | therefore |

## Present tense -re verbs   ≫ Page 90

Use the present tense to talk about what is happening NOW or happens REGULARLY.

| | |
|---|---|
| vendre | to sell |
| je vends | sell |
| tu vends | you sell |
| il / elle / on vend | he / she / one sells |

J'attends avec impatience l'arrivée de mes commandes.
I am waiting impatiently for my purchases to arrive.

## Worked example   LISTENING 33   target C

Listen. Which comment does Vincent make?
E

A  There is a risk of losing your money.
B  You can get some good bargains.
C  I don't shop online.
D  It means I don't have to go to the shops.
E  I have problems with having things delivered.
F  I always use well-known firms.

– Vincent?
– Moi, j'adore ça, avec ma carte de crédit c'est très facile. À mon avis, de nos jours, il n'y a pas de risques. Le problème pour moi, c'est qu'il n'y a jamais personne à la maison pour la livraison.

## EXAM ALERT!

Option A was the most commonly incorrect answer for this question, even though Vincent says **il n'y a pas de risques** (there are no risks). Students had to recognise negatives to get the answer correct.

> This was a real exam question that a lot of students struggled with – be prepared!   Result Plus

Vincent uses two negatives together: **ne ... jamais** = never and **ne ... personne** = nobody (there is never anybody at home). If you hear these, you will be guided to the correct answer, E. If you don't hear the negative, you may well end up choosing the incorrect answer.

## Now try this   LISTENING 34   target C

Listen to three more people and write the correct letter from the comments above for each one.

1  Orphélie
2  Samir
3  Benita

Don't miss the negatives!

# Shopping preferences

You may choose to do a presentation on shopping. Be prepared to answer questions after your presentation.

## Shopping: Les préférences

| | |
|---|---|
| avoir plus de choix | to have more choice |
| donner | to give |
| emprunter | to borrow |
| essayer | to try (on) |
| faire la queue | to queue |
| préférer | to prefer |
| de bon marché | good value for money |
| démodé(e) / rétro | old-fashioned |
| pas cher / chère | cheap |
| soldé | reduced |
| boutique de mode (f) | fashion boutique |
| sélection (f) | selection / choice |
| service (m) | service |
| soldes d'été (mpl) | summer sales |
| Ça m'est égal! | I don't care! |
| Ce n'est pas grand-chose. | It's no big deal. |
| J'en ai marre! | I'm sick of it! |
| Je m'en fous! | I couldn't care less! |

## Verbs with à

| | |
|---|---|
| aller à | to go to |
| Je vais aux magasins. | I go to the shops. |
| à + les = aux | |
| jouer à | to play (+ sport / activity) |
| Je joue au football. | I play football. |
| à + le = au | |
| s'intéresser à | to be interested in |

Je m'intéresse à la mode.
I am interested in fashion.
Je m'y intéresse.
I'm interested in it.

---

## Worked example 🗣 SPEAKING

Où préfères-tu acheter tes vêtements?

> Moi, je préfère acheter mes vêtements dans les grands magasins. Il y a plus de choix et les prix sont moins chers. J'aime y aller avec mes copines le week-end.

**AIMING HIGHER**

> Je ne m'intéresse pas aux magasins et les vêtements ne m'intéressent pas non plus! Je n'ai jamais acheté de vêtement de marque. Quand j'ai besoin de vêtements, ma mère me les achète au supermarché. Je vais sur Internet. J'y préfère faire tous mes achats. J'aimerais un nouveau jeu vidéo alors je le chercherai en ligne.

## Speaking strategies

- Use filler words, *euh* (er), *ben* (well), *et alors* (and so), *et puis* (and then) to slow you down.
- If you don't understand a question, ask: *Pouvez-vous répéter, s'il vous plaît?* (Can you repeat that, please?) BUT don't ask after every question.

**CONTROLLED ASSESSMENT**

You will be asked questions in your speaking assessment, so make sure you prepare answers to possible questions for your chosen topics.

Always listen carefully to the questions you are asked and do not just repeat an answer you have learned in advance if it does NOT answer the question.

---

## Now try this 🗣 SPEAKING

Prepare a 30-second answer to the question: Où préfères-tu acheter tes vêtements?

# At the train station

If you are describing a journey for a writing assessment, using the time expressions on this page will help raise your level.

## À la gare

| | |
|---|---|
| d'abord | first of all |
| puis | then |
| par conséquent | therefore |
| ensuite | next |
| enfin | at last |
| finalement | finally |
| comme d'habitude | as usual |
| quand | when |
| quai (m) | platform |
| wagon (m) | carriage |
| place (f) | seat |
| s'ennuyer | to be bored |
| se fâcher | to be cross |
| s'installer | to sit down |
| se presser/se dépêcher | to hurry |
| se tromper de | to be mistaken |

### Reflexive verbs

Page 94

Some verbs need an extra me, te, se, etc.

| | | |
|---|---|---|
| je + me | je me lève | I get up |
| tu + te | tu te lèves | you get up |
| il(s) / elle(s) + se | il / elle se lève | he / she gets up |

Reflexive verbs take être in the perfect tense.

The past participle has to agree with the subject.

| | |
|---|---|
| Je me suis fâché(e). | I got angry. |
| Tu t'es ennuyé(e). | You got bored. |
| Elle s'est trompée. | She made a mistake. |

Je me suis dépêché(e) pour le train.
I hurried to get the train.

---

## Worked example

WRITING

Do you travel by train?

Je n'aime pas prendre le train.

D'abord, il faut admettre que je n'aime pas prendre le train.

**AIMING HIGHER**

L'autre jour je suis arrivé à la gare, comme d'habitude, en retard. Par conséquent j'ai dû me dépêcher et je me suis trompé de quai. Quand je me suis finalement installé à ma place, quelqu'un est venu me dire que ce n'était pas ma place. Je m'étais trompé de wagon.

• Simple sentences can always be improved and developed!

• Look how the addition of d'abord (first of all) and an explanation: il faut admettre que (I must admit that) raises the level.

Look at how the rest of the story is improved by adding these expressions:

| | |
|---|---|
| l'autre jour | the other day |
| comme d'habitude | as usual |
| par conséquent | as a consequence / therefore |
| quand   when | finalement   finally. |

---

## Now try this

WRITING

Write a paragraph of about 60 words giving your opinion of travelling by train.

Make sure you use at least two **tenses** and some of the **time expressions** from this page.

# Money

Use this page to revise money vocabulary as well as how to use the near future to express what you are 'going to' do.

## L'argent

| | |
|---|---|
| argent liquide (m) | cash |
| carte bancaire (f) | bank card |
| carte de crédit (f) | credit card |
| chèque de voyage (m) | traveller's cheque |
| billet de 10€ (m) | 10€ note |
| pièce (de 2€) (f) | (2€) coin |
| euro (m) | euro |
| cent (m) | cent |
| livre (m) | pound (sterling) |
| monnaie (f) | change (coins) |
| changer de l'argent | to change money |
| dépenser de l'argent | to spend money |
| toucher un chèque | to cash a cheque |
| cours de change (m) | exchange rate |
| faute (f) | mistake |
| problème (m) | problem |
| compte (m) | account |

## Near future

 Page 98

Use part of aller (to go) + infinitive to say what you are going to do soon.

Nous allons chercher une banque.
We are going to look for a bank.

Ils vont mettre de l'argent de côté.
They are going to save some money.

Je vais changer de l'argent.
I am going to change some money.

## Worked example  LISTENING 35  target D

What does the speaker say?    C

A  I need to give my husband 50€.
B  My husband bought me a 50€ purse.
C  We are having a problem at the car park.
D  We need to go to the lost property office.
E  I have only got foreign money left.

– Avez-vous de la monnaie?
Nous en avons besoin pour
le parking et je n'ai
qu'un billet de 50€.

je n'ai qu' =
I have **only** got

## Listening strategies

- The listening passages in the exam are not very long so make sure you really concentrate on every word to find the answers.

- Jot down any answers you are unsure of in pencil on the first listening, then check them to confirm or change them on a second listening.

- The recording will carry on to the next activity after the second listening, so make sure you are not still trying to change answers then.

- Don't confuse similar words such as monnaie (cash) and porte-monnaie (purse – literally 'money carrier').

## Now try this  LISTENING 36  target D

Listen to three more people and match their money problems to the correct statements above.

1 ☐        2 ☐        3 ☐

# Travel problems

You may choose to write about a problem journey for your assessment. Remember to include adverbs if you can.

## Problèmes de voyage

| | |
|---|---|
| aller-retour (m) | return ticket |
| aller-simple (m) | single ticket |
| billetterie automatique (f) | ticket machine |
| distributeur automatique (m) | ticket machine |
| correspondance (f) | connection |
| retard (m) | delay |
| guichet (m) | ticket office |
| occupé(e) | taken (seat) |
| place (f) | seat |
| portière (f) | door (of train) |
| prix des billets / tarif (m) | fare |
| voie (f) | track |
| être en panne | to be broken down |
| être en retard | to be late |
| manquer le train | to miss the train |
| monter dans un train | to get on a train |
| embêtant(e) | annoying |
| il y a du monde | it's busy / crowded |

## Adverbs

Page 85

Adverbs describe verbs: walk QUICKLY, read SLOWLY.

Here are some useful adverbs.

- vite — quickly
- vraiment — truly, really
- pire — worse
- bien — well
- mieux — better
- lentement — slowly
- mal — badly
- rapidement — rapidly
- seulement — only
- heureusement — happily, fortunately

adverbs

---

## Worked example

**WRITING**

Write about a train journey.

Heureusement je suis arrivé à la gare en avance. Malheureusement la billetterie automatique était en panne et j'ai dû faire la queue à la caisse.

**AIMING HIGHER**

La semaine dernière, je suis rentré de Londres en train. C'était vraiment embêtant. Il y avait beaucoup de monde et toutes les places étaient occupées, alors j'ai dû rester debout. Il y avait des travaux sur la voie donc le train devait rouler lentement et il s'est arrêté à chaque petite gare en route. Nous avions une demi-heure de retard et mon père m'attendait à la gare. Il n'était pas content.

- Use heureusement (fortunately) and malheureusement (unfortunately) to show two opposite opinions or pros and cons.

- If you are writing about towns, use the French name where possible: Londres (London), Genève (Geneva), Bruxelles (Brussels).

- Make sure you get your **adjective agreements** correct – it is vital in order to get a top grade.

- This text also contains a variety of **interesting vocabulary**. Although you can use a dictionary in the exam, it's best to look up words in advance and use them with confidence.

---

## Now try this

**WRITING**

Add as many **adverbs** as possible!

Write 100 words about a train journey you took which went wrong.

# Lost property

If you are preparing a photo-based discussion, the loss of something may be a good, more unusual topic to choose.

## Au bureau des objets trouvés

| | |
|---|---|
| appareil-photo (m) | camera |
| carte d'identité (f) | identity card |
| chat / chien (m) | cat / dog |
| clefs / clés (fpl) | keys |
| montre (f) | watch |
| paquet (m) | packet |
| parapluie (m) | umbrella |
| portefeuille (m) | wallet |
| en coton / laine | cotton / wool |
| J'ai perdu mon portable. | I have lost my phone. |
| Je ne trouve plus mes gants. | I can't find my gloves. |
| Ma bicyclette a disparu. | My bike has disappeared. |
| Il / Elle est bleu(e) / en cuir. | It is blue / made of leather. |
| Il me fallait aller au commissariat. | I had to go to the police station. |
| J'ai dû remplir une fiche. | I had to fill in a form. |
| J'étais triste / traumatisé(e). | I was sad / shocked. |
| C'est / C'était dommage. | It is / was a pity. |

## Using qui and que

Page 88

qui = who / that

que = which / that / whom

C'est ma mère qui a perdu sa carte de crédit.

It's my mother who has lost her credit card.

Elle était dans un sac à provisions que j'ai laissé dans le bus.

It was in a shopping bag which I left on the bus.

Choosing a photo? Choose one you WANT to talk about and which will help to make your discussion a truly individual one!

## Worked example

**SPEAKING**

Pourquoi as-tu choisi cette photo?

J'ai choisi cette photo de mon petit chat, qui s'appelle Maxi, parce qu'il a disparu. Hier il était à la maison toute la journée et il est sorti le soir, comme d'habitude attraper des souris, mais ce matin il n'est pas rentré. Il faut le chercher!

### CONTROLLED ASSESSMENT

Think of plenty of questions you might be asked about your photo, and the answers you would give.

Just as in a presentation, you need to make sure you use a variety of **tenses**, **opinions** and a wide variety of complex **structures** and interesting **vocabulary**.

## Now try this

**SPEAKING**

Choose a photo of something you have lost and prepare a discussion about it by answering these questions.

- Pourquoi avez-vous choisi cette photo?
- Vous l'avez perdu quand et où?
- Est-ce que vous pouvez le décrire?
- Pourquoi est-ce qu'il est important pour vous?

# Problems

Including a problem aspect in your presentation will help you use some more complex structures and tenses, such as the pluperfect.

## Les problèmes

| | |
|---|---|
| Je voulais me plaindre. | I wanted to complain. |
| Je suis déçu(e). | I am disappointed. |
| Je suis désolé(e). | I'm sorry. |
| J'ai appelé le magasin. | I rang the shop. |
| Je voudrais parler au patron / à la patronne. | I would like to speak to the boss. |
| On a appelé l'agent de sécurité. | Someone called the security guard. |
| On a appelé mes parents. | They called my parents. |
| J'ai dû aller à la gendarmerie. | I had to go to the police station. |
| Je n'en savais rien. | I didn't know anything about it. |
| C'était le comble. | It was the last straw. |
| Sans rien me dire. | Without saying anything to me. |

## Pluperfect tense

Page 100

Pluperfect tense = HAD done something = imperfect form of avoir / être + past participle

J'avais acheté une carte. I had bought a card.
Elle y était allée en bus.  She had gone by bus.

| | | |
|---|---|---|
| j'avais | | |
| tu avais | joué | had played |
| il / elle / on avait | | |
| j'étais | | |
| tu étais | rentré(e) | had returned |
| il / elle / on était | | |

J'avais déjà mangé un croque-monsieur quand ma mère m'a donné une crêpe!

## Worked example 🔊 SPEAKING

Décris un problème.

J'aimerais pouvoir oublier ce jour-là. Dimanche dernier c'était la fête des Mères et le samedi je suis allé en ville avec mes copains. Nous sommes allés chercher des cartes et des petits cadeaux pour nos mères.

Je n'ai jamais beaucoup d'argent et j'avais déjà acheté une carte, par conséquent je n'ai rien acheté mais je suis resté avec les autres pendant qu'ils choisissaient des cadeaux.

Sans rien me dire, un de mes copains a glissé une bouteille de parfum dans mon sac. Je n'en savais rien mais quand on est sorti du magasin, l'alarme a sonné … Quelle horreur!

## Aiming higher

Tips for improving your presentation.

1. Start with an idiom: J'aimerais pouvoir oublier ce jour-là. = I would like to be able to forget that day.

2. Bring other people into your story to avoid just using the je form.

3. Add cultural references, such as la fête des Mères (Mother's Day) used here.

4. Include plenty of tenses in your story (present, past and pluperfect) if you're aiming for the very top grades.

5. Make sure you use je suis / j'étais + past participle for verbs which need it (see page 100).

6. Include drama in your presentation to increase interest levels, e.g. l'alarme a sonné = the alarm sounded.

## Now try this 🔊 SPEAKING

Do you want to know what happened next? Finish the story in about 60 words!

# School subjects

You need to be able to talk about your school subjects, give your opinions and justify them.

## Les matières

J'apprends / J'étudie ...    I learn / I study ...

J'aime / Je préfère ...    I like / I prefer ...

Je n'aime pas ...    I don't like ...

l'allemand (m)

l'anglais (m)

l'espagnol (m)

le français (m)

la biologie (f)

la chimie (f)

la physique (f)

les maths (fpl)

l'informatique (f)

la géographie

l'histoire (f)

l'EPS / éducation physique (f)

### Negative sentences

After the negative ne ... pas, use de before the noun.

Je ne fais pas de gymnastique.
I don't do gymnastics.

Je n'ai pas de cours le mercredi.
I don't have lessons on Wednesdays.

### depuis + present tense

depuis + present tense = how long you have been doing something

J'apprends le français depuis quatre ans.
I have been learning French for four years.

EPS 'e' is pronounced 'uh': 'uh pay ess'.
EMT – 'uh em tay'. (This is DT in English.)
Subject names are often abbreviated: techno, info, bio, géo.

---

## Worked example

Tu aimes quelles matières?

J'étudie les maths, les sciences et l'anglais. Ma matière préférée c'est l'EPS parce que c'est intéressant.

Don't just give a long list of subjects. Give a couple, and then move on to a new construction.

**AIMING HIGHER** Personnellement je n'aime pas trop l'EMT parce que je ne m'y intéresse pas, ce n'est pas mon truc. En revanche, j'adore le sport. C'est rigolo et d'habitude on en fait deux heures par semaine. Mon sport préféré c'est le basket et ce qu'il y a de mieux, c'est qu'on peut y jouer dans une équipe, même si on n'est pas très doué. Quand j'irai au lycée, je vais continuer le basket mais j'espère aussi faire de l'escalade.

This student expresses a range of **ideas** and **points of view** as well as using more than one **tense**. There is a variety of interesting vocabulary and structures, including the adverbs **personnellement**, **d'habitude, trop** ... and the phrases **en revanche** (on the other hand), **ce n'est pas mon truc** (it's not my thing), **ce qu'il y a de mieux, c'est** (the best thing is).

---

## Now try this

Say a couple of sentences to answer each of these questions.

- Quel est ta matière préféreé? Pourquoi?
- Est-ce qu'il y a une matière que tu n'aimes pas?

# School life

You will often have to understand opinions about school in listening tasks.

## La vie au collège

J'ai trop de devoirs. ☹  I have too much homework.

Le professeur est sympa.  The teacher is nice.

Je déteste les contrôles.  I hate tests.

Les examens sont durs.  Exams are hard.

Mes notes sont bonnes.  My marks are good.

J'aime les langues étrangères. ☺  I like foreign languages.

Les arts ménagers, c'est nul.  Cookery is rubbish.

J'adore l'étude des médias.  I love media studies.

Je suis fort(e) en maths.  I am strong in maths.

Il est faible en dessin.  He is weak at art.

Le prof de sciences physiques explique bien.
The chemistry and physics teacher explains it well.

La journée scolaire est longue.
The school day is long.

## 'first', 'second', 'third'

premier is the only ordinal number to change in the feminine form:

|     | masculine | feminine |
|-----|-----------|----------|
| 1st | premier   | première |
| 2nd | deuxième  | deuxième |
| 3rd | troisième | troisième |

le premier cours   the first lesson

la première leçon   the first lesson

Je suis en ...
I am in ...

sixième — Yr 7
cinquième — Yr 8
quatrième — Yr 9
troisième — Yr 10
seconde — Yr 11
première — Yr 12
terminale — Yr 13

---

## Worked example  LISTENING 37  target B

Who says what about school?

Write the name of the correct person.

Roxanne  Hubert  Justine

(a) Who says their school is well equipped?
    Roxanne
(b) Who likes school because he / she sees friends there?
(c) Who doesn't mind having a long school day?
(d) Who thinks most of his / her teachers are good?
(e) Who thinks homework is useful?

– Écoutons d'abord Roxanne.

– Mon école est très bien équipée. Je l'aime bien mais la journée scolaire est trop longue. La plupart de mes profs expliquent bien mais ils donnent trop de devoirs! Le soir je n'ai pas le temps de voir mes amis.

## EXAM ALERT!

In this task you have to distinguish between the main points, details and opinions. Many students found the three passages quite challenging.

This was a real exam question that a lot of students struggled with – **be prepared!**  ResultsPlus

- Listen **carefully** from the very beginning – if you miss the speaker's name, you won't be able to match the sentences.
- Make sure you read all the statements **before** you listen – that way you can match the people to the sentences more easily.
- Here, it is not enough to identify a key word in the recording. You also need to identify the **opinion** that goes with it.
- All three speakers mention **les devoirs** (homework) but you are only interested in the person who finds it **useful** (question e).

## Now try this  LISTENING 38  target B

Listen to the whole recording and complete the activity above.

# School routine

You may need to write about school routine in your writing assessment. Make sure your verbs are correct.

## La routine au collège

| | |
|---|---|
| commencer / débuter | to begin |
| finir | to finish |
| durer | to last |
| fréquenter l'école | to attend school |
| le matin | in the morning |
| l'après-midi | in the afternoon |
| cours (m) / leçon (f) | lesson |
| récréation / récré (f) | break |
| heure du déjeuner (f) | lunch break |
| retenue (f) | detention |
| pas d'école | no school |
| semestre (m) | semester |
| trimestre (m) | term |
| grandes vacances (fpl) | summer holidays |
| rentrée (f) | start of the new school year |

## Third person plural

The third person singular (he / she) and plural (they) of most verbs sound the same but have to be SPELLED correctly to score highly:

| singular (he) | plural (they) |
|---|---|
| il commence | ils commencent |
| il rentre | ils rentrent |

Irregular third person forms:

| aller | to go | ils vont | they go |
|---|---|---|---|
| avoir | to have | ils ont | they have |
| être | to be | ils sont | they are |
| faire | to do | ils font | they do |

Les cours finissent à quatre heures.
Lessons finish at four o'clock.

## Worked example

Describe your typical school day.

Le matin les cours commencent à huit heures et finissent à midi vingt. Un cours dure une heure. Nous avons une heure quarante pour le déjeuner et puis les cours recommencent à deux heures.

This is adequate, but is all in one tense. If you are aiming for a higher grade you need to use a **past** or **future** tense as well, and include an **opinion**.

**AIMING HIGHER**

Le mardi, les cours ne commencent qu'à dix heures. Les élèves comme moi, qui prennent un car de ramassage, arrivent au collège à huit heures. Pendant la récré, on va normalement dans la cour pour bavarder, mais hier je suis allée à la bibliothèque parce qu'il me fallait finir mes devoirs de dessin. Je déteste le dessin parce que je trouve les devoirs très difficiles et ennuyeux.

- This uses an interesting structure to begin with: **les cours ne commencent qu'à** (lessons don't begin until), which makes an excellent start. It also includes the **perfect** tense by describing a specific event from yesterday.
- The use of the expression **il me fallait** (I had to) + infinitive is the sort of structure that will help if you're aiming for a top grade.

## Now try this

Write a paragraph of about 60 to 100 words about your school routine.
- When do lessons start / finish?
- What do you do at break / lunch time?

# Comparing schools

Be prepared to compare French and English schools if you are talking about school in a speaking assessment.

## Une comparaison des collèges

| | |
|---|---|
| brevet (m) | exam taken at 15 |
| bac (m) | exam taken at 18 |
| diplôme (m) | qualification |
| bulletin scolaire (m) | school report |
| école (f) | school |
| collège (d'enseignement secondaire) / CES (m) | secondary school |
| maternelle (f) | nursery school |
| lycée d'enseignement professionel / LEP (m) | vocational school |
| école privée (f) | private school |
| lycée (m) | sixth form |
| échouer à un examen | to fail an exam |
| passer un examen | to sit an exam (NOT pass an exam) |
| réussir à un examen | to pass an exam |
| en principe | as a rule |
| moins / plus difficile | less / more difficult |

### Adjective agreements  ≫ Page 81

| singular | | plural | |
|---|---|---|---|
| masc | fem | masc | fem |
| court | courte | courts | courtes |
| long | longue | longs | longues |
| actif | active | actifs | actives |

La journée est plus longue.
The day is longer.

Les grandes vacances sont moins longues.
The summer holidays are shorter.

Les cours sont intéressants.

## Worked example 🔊 SPEAKING

Faites une comparaison des collèges anglais et français.

En France, en principe, les collèges sont plus grands que les collèges en Angleterre. Il y a plus d'élèves et plus de profs. Je préfère aller au collège en Angleterre parce qu'en France on doit aller à l'école le samedi matin. Je détesterais ça!

Remember to give your opinion, and try to use a simple conditional expression: **Je détesterais ça!** (I would hate that!)

**AIMING HIGHER** En Angleterre, je trouve que c'est mieux parce que la journée scolaire est moins longue qu'en France. Selon moi, les élèves français commencent trop tôt. Mais en Angleterre, il faut porter un uniforme et à mon avis c'est stupide. En France c'est mieux, on porte ce qu'on veut. L'année dernière, je suis allée voir mon correspondant à Lille et je l'ai accompagné au collège.

- Use lots of opinion phrases to help your presentation flow well.
- Use pronouns rather than repeating nouns to make your speech flow better – **je l'ai accompagné** (I accompanied him).
- Include a personal experience at the end to allow you to use the perfect tense.

## Now try this ✎ WRITING

Write 100 words about things which you think are different, better or worse in your school system, compared with the French system.

# Primary school

Talking about what you used to do at primary school is a good way of introducing the imperfect tense.

## L'école primaire

| instituteur (m) / institutrice (f) | teacher (primary) |
|---|---|
| Quand j'étais petit(e) … | When I was small … |
| j'allais à l'école à pied. | I walked to school. |
| j'avais un petit cartable. | I had a small school bag. |
| je mangeais à la cantine. | I ate at the canteen. |
| on s'amusait mieux. | we had more fun. |
| on avait moins de contrôles. | we had fewer tests. |
| on faisait des promenades en été. | we used to go for walks in the summer. |

> **Imperfect tense** 》 Page 97
>
> IMPERFECT tense = what USED to happen
>
> Je jouais au foot.
> I used to play football.
>
> Quand j'avais huit ans.
> When I was eight.
>
> On dessinait.
> We used to draw.

Je jouais au foot dans la cour de récréation.
I played football in the playground.

Les profs n'étaient pas sévères.
The teachers weren't strict.

On chantait et dessinait tous les jours.
We used to sing and draw every day.

---

## Worked example — READING — target A

Put a cross next to the correct answer.

Quand Timothé était plus jeune …

A  il ne faisait pas ce que l'institutrice lui demandait à l'école.  ☒

B  il était un bon élève.  ☐

C  il n'allait pas à l'école maternelle.  ☐

> Moi, j'étais toujours très sage à l'école maternelle, mais Timothé ne voulait jamais faire ce qu'on lui demandait! Mes parents disaient à Timothé d'être comme moi. Papa rigolait quand je faisais une bêtise, alors qu'avec Timothé, il s'énervait!

### EXAM ALERT!

Good comprehension skills are needed here, as is an ability to draw conclusions from the text as a whole. The task is made harder, as the questions are in French and not phrased in identical ways to material in the text.

> Students have struggled with exam questions similar to this – **be prepared!**   ResultsPlus

Don't be put off by the use of a different tense in a reading text. Here, the imperfect forms are similar to their present tense forms and infinitives: **voulait – vouloir** (to want).

---

## Now try this — READING — target A

Put a cross next to the correct answer.

À cause de Timothé, son père …

A  était fier.  ☐     B  était toujours content.  ☐     C  se fâchait.  ☐

> Remember to put a cross and not a tick!

# Issues at school

Make sure you can use the vocabulary on this page to talk about issues at school.
Say, too, whether you think rules are fair (justes) or unfair (injustes).

## Problèmes au collège

| Il faut ... | You have to ... |
| --- | --- |
| bien se tenir en classe. | behave well in class. |
| éteindre son portable. | switch off your mobile. |
| être poli(e) / respectueux/euse. | be polite / respectful. |
| faire attention aux profs. | pay attention to the teachers. |

| Il est interdit de ... | You are not allowed to ... |
| --- | --- |
| courir dans les couloirs. | run in the corridors. |
| fumer (dans les vestiaires). | smoke (in the changing rooms). |
| mâcher du chewing-gum. | chew gum. |
| porter des boucles d'oreille. | wear earrings. |
| utiliser son portable en classe. | use your mobile in class. |

## Il faut + infinitive

il faut + infinitive = HAVE to / MUST do something

Il faut être à l'heure.
You have to be on time.

il ne faut pas + infinitive = MUST NOT do something

Il ne faut pas fumer.   You mustn't smoke.

Use the IMPERFECT tense to talk about things you had to do:

Il fallait travailler dur.
You had to work hard.

- Other ways of saying you are NOT ALLOWED to do something:

  Il est défendu de courir dans les couloirs.
  It is forbidden to run in the corridors.

  Il est interdit de dire des gros mots.
  Swearing is not allowed.

---

## Worked example

READING  target **C**

Which sign matches which person?

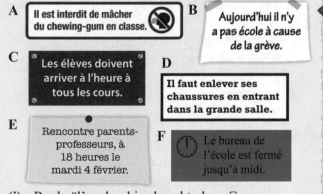

A  **Il est interdit de mâcher du chewing-gum en classe.** 🚫

B  Aujourd'hui il n'y a pas école à cause de la grève.

C  Les élèves doivent arriver à l'heure à tous les cours.

D  Il faut enlever ses chaussures en entrant dans la grande salle.

E  Rencontre parents-professeurs, à 18 heures le mardi 4 février.

F  🕐 Le bureau de l'école est fermé jusqu'à midi.

(i)   Raphaël's school is closed today.  B
(ii)  Lilou must get to lessons on time.
(iii) The school office is closed.
(iv)  Pupils must take their shoes off in the hall.
(v)   Baptiste's parents are due at school this evening.

## EXAM ALERT!

Some students panic when they don't understand words. Here, even if you didn't know that **en grève** meant on strike, you can still answer B if you spot the word **pas** (no) + **école** (school) = no school.

Students have struggled with exam questions similar to this – be prepared!  Results**Plus**

## Reading exam tip

Look through all the questions and do the ones you're confident about first. Then come back to the others. Never leave a gap – always have a go, even if you're not sure.

---

## Now try this

READING  target **C**

Complete the activity above.

# Future plans

Using the conditional tense is a straightforward way of expressing your wishes for what you want to do next in education.

## Projets de l'avenir

| Je voudrais ... | I would like to ... |
|---|---|
| réussir à mon brevet. | pass my (GCSE) exams. |
| entrer en première. | go to the sixth form. |
| continuer mes études. | continue studying. |
| étudier la sociologie. | study sociology. |
| préparer le bac. | study for (A level) exams. |
| aller à l'université. | go to university. |
| chercher un emploi. | look for a job. |
| faire du bénévolat. | do volunteering. |
| faire un apprentissage. | do an apprenticeship. |
| redoubler. | repeat the year. |
| gagner de l'argent. | earn some money. |
| aller voir le conseiller / la conseillère. d'orientation. | go and see the careers adviser. |
| réussir. | be successful. |

### Conditional tense
Page 99

To say what you WOULD LIKE to do, use a conditional verb + infinitive.

| Je voudrais | I would like to |
|---|---|
| J'aimerais | I would like to |
| Je préférerais | I would prefer to |
| Je pourrais | I would be able to |

J'aimerais voyager à l'étranger.
I would like to travel abroad.
Je voudrais être médecin.
I would like to be a doctor.

Je voudrais étudier l'anglais et l'histoire à l'université.

---

## Worked example  WRITING

Write about your future education plans.

Après le brevet, je voudrais aller en première et préparer mon bac. Après le bac, j'aimerais bien trouver un emploi. J'aimerais aller à l'université mais je crois que ça coûte trop cher.

This answer uses **present** and **conditional** tenses, but with a limited range of vocabulary – a few **adjectives** would have improved the work.

Using the conjunction **mais** (but) is a good way to join sentences and make the text flow better.

**AIMING HIGHER**

Je voudrais réussir à mon bac et aller à l'université. Je préférerais étudier à Paris parce que j'ai beaucoup de copains qui y habitent et j'adore la ville. En ce moment, je pense que j'aimerais prendre une année sabbatique pour faire du bénévolat en Afrique. Ça m'intéresserait beaucoup car j'aimerais bien aider les gens, surtout les enfants.

This account is a coherent piece of writing using different tenses and a variety of structures.

It avoids overusing **parce que** by including the alternative **car**.

**qui y habitent** (who live there) is a good relative pronoun construction with the pronoun **y** (there).

année sabbatique = gap year

---

## Now try this  WRITING

Write six sentences saying what your future plans are.

Use the following expressions:
Je voudrais        J'aimerais
Je préférerais     Je pourrais

# In the future

Using the FUTURE TENSE correctly will help you do well when discussing future plans.

## À l'avenir

| | |
|---|---|
| Quand je quitterai le collège ... | When I leave school ... |
| Après avoir quitté le collège ... | After I have left school ... |
| je chercherai un emploi. | I will look for a job. |
| j'étudierai l'économie à l'université. | I will study economics at university. |
| je ferai une licence de commerce. | I will do a degree in business studies. |
| je ferai un apprentissage. | I will do an apprenticeship. |
| j'apprendrai à construire des maisons. | I will learn to build houses. |
| je voyagerai. | I will see the world. |
| je commencerai ma carrière. | I will start my career. |
| j'aurai ma propre entreprise. | I will have my own firm. |
| je serai riche. | I will be rich. |

## Future tense

Page 98

Learn and use the following future tense verbs and phrases. The first one is a regular –er verb; the rest are irregular.

| | |
|---|---|
| je jouerai | I will play |
| j'irai | I will go |
| j'aurai | I will have |
| je serai | I will be |
| je ferai | I will make / do |
| je verrai | I will see |

Je ferai le tour du monde.    Je serai footballeur professionel.

---

## Worked example    LISTENING 38    target D

Who wants to do what?

Put the correct letter in the box.

| Enzo | D |
| Lola | ☐ |
| Éva | ☐ |
| Maël | ☐ |
| Yanis | ☐ |

A  Travel
B  Be a pop star
C  Don't know
D  Apprenticeship
E  Study music
F  Buy a car

– Enzo?
– Je ferai un apprentissage dans une entreprise en ville.

## Listening tips

- Read the answer choices BEFORE you listen and think about which French words you might hear.
- You don't need to understand EVERY word the speakers say, but you do need to know what the KEY items of vocabulary are.

- Here, Enzo mentions un apprentissage which leads you directly to answer D: Apprenticeship. It doesn't matter if you don't catch dans une entreprise en ville.
- If you didn't know that un apprentissage means apprenticeship, then dans une entreprise en ville (in a company in town) can still lead you to the answer.

## Now try this    LISTENING 40    target D

Listen to the rest of the recording and complete the task above.

# Jobs

Use the vocabulary on this page to say what jobs your family members do.

## Les métiers

| | |
|---|---|
| agent de police | police officer |
| architecte (m) | architect |
| boucher / ère | butcher |
| boulanger / ère | baker |
| caissier / ière | cashier |
| charpentier (m) | carpenter |
| chauffeur (de camion) (m) | (lorry) driver |
| cuisinier / ière | cook |
| facteur / trice | postman / woman |
| fermier / ière | farmer |
| fonctionnaire | civil servant |
| gendarme / policier | police officer |
| steward / hôtesse de l'air | air steward |
| informaticien(ne) | computer scientist |
| ingénieur(e) | engineer |
| maçon (m) | builder |
| médecin / docteur | doctor |
| pharmacien(ne) | pharmacist |
| plombier | plumber |
| pompier | firefighter |
| secrétaire | secretary |
| vétérinaire | vet |

Il est homme d'affaires.    He is a businessman.

Elle est femme d'affaires.    She is a businesswoman.

### Masculine and feminine forms

Il est infirmier. Elle est infirmière.
He / She is a nurse.

Il est vendeur. Elle est vendeuse.
He / She is a sales assistant.

Il est facteur.    Il est fermier.
Elle est factrice.    Elle est fermière.

Look for words like English words (cognates):
infirmier works in an infirmary = nurse
coiffeur/euse is like coiffure (hairstyle) = hairdresser
mécanicien, électricien, journaliste and fleuriste look and sound familiar.

## Worked example 🎧41 target C

Answer the question in English.
What is Tom's dad's job?   sales assistant

– Que font tes parents?
– Mon père est vendeur dans un hypermarché.

- Read the question carefully – you need to listen for a **job word**, not an opinion or any details about the job, but the job itself.
- Answer in **English** if asked to – not in French. Writing **vendeur** would be incorrect – you have to give the English term salesman / sales assistant.

## Now try this 🎧42 target C

Listen to the whole recording and answer these questions.

1 Why is Tom's dad's job tiring?
2 What is Tom's mum's job?
3 Where does she work ?
4 What is her opinion of her job?
5 What is Tom's stepmum's job?
6 How many days a week does she work?

Read the questions carefully so that you write the correct answer, and not just everything you hear!

# Job adverts

Job adverts may well crop up in your reading exam, so learn the vocabulary on this page.

## Offres d'emploi

| | |
|---|---|
| au chômage | unemployed |
| en grève | on strike |
| employé(e) (m/f) | employee |
| employeur / euse (m/f) | employer |
| collègue (m/f) | colleague |
| conditions de travail (fpl) | working conditions |
| gagner un salaire | to earn a wage |
| bien / mal payé(e) | well / badly paid |
| 20 euros de l'heure | 20 euros per hour |
| travail (m) | work |
| travail à plein temps | full-time work |
| travail à temps partiel | part-time work |
| travail par roulement | shiftwork |
| Je voudrais travailler ... | I would like to work ... |
|    en entreprise |    for a firm |
|    dans un bureau |    in an office |

## Prepositions

Page 103

Prepositions are SMALL words which give BIG information about where, how and when things happen.

| | | | |
|---|---|---|---|
| à | at, to | de | from, of |
| après | after | en | in, by |
| avec | with | pour | for |
| dans | in | sans | without |
| heures de travail | working hours | | |
| dans une usine | in a factory | | |
| à domicile | from home | | |
| en plein air | in the open air | | |
| après une semaine | after a week | | |

avec enthousiasme
with enthusiasm

---

## Worked example

READING   target C

Read this advert.

**On cherche des animateurs / animatrices pour clubs de vacances. Vous ...**
- voulez travailler avec des enfants ou des ados?
- travaillez avec enthousiasme?
- n'avez pas peur de travail en plein air?

Nous avons des centres à la montagne, au bord de la mer et à l'étranger.
Après une semaine de formation, on vous envoie au centre qui correspond le mieux à vos aptitudes.

Put a cross in the correct box.

This is an advert for ...

A   animators ☐
B   holiday club instructors ☒
C   nursery workers ☐

## Reading tips

- Questions on a text usually follow the SAME ORDER as the text itself, so you won't find the first answer at the end of the extract.
- READ the question and all its answer options and then look for the key words for each answer.
- Don't be misled by FALSE FRIENDS. Here animateurs / animatrices are NOT animators, but instructors.
- USE all the words in the text to make sure of your answers – the words clubs de vacances will put you on the right track here to holiday club instructors, answer B.

---

## Now try this

READING   target C

Look again at the job advert. Choose the correct answer.

(a) The firm is looking for **intelligent / keen / sporty** employees.
(b) You must be prepared to work **nights / abroad / outdoors**.
(c) The training lasts **three / five / seven** days.
(d) You are sent to the **nearest / most suitable / best** club.

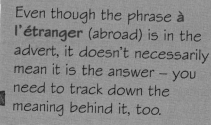

Even though the phrase à l'étranger (abroad) is in the advert, it doesn't necessarily mean it is the answer – you need to track down the meaning behind it, too.

# Writing a CV

You may meet a CV in a reading exam, or use part of it for a writing assessment, but avoid long lists and very short sentences.

## CV

| | |
|---|---|
| apprenti(e) (m/f) | apprentice |
| bulletin scolaire (m) | school report |
| certificat de travail (m) | certificate of employment |
| ci-inclus, ci-joint | enclosed |
| formation / éducation (f) | education |
| stage de (voile) (m) | (sailing) course |
| expérience (du travail) (f) | experience (of work) |
| joindre | to enclose, attach |
| expérimenté(e) | experienced |
| qualifié(e) | qualified |
| réussir | to be successful in |

### Dates

Make sure you are confident with saying the years in French.

Je suis né(e) en mille-neuf-cent-quatre-vingt-dix à Hull.
I was born in 1990 in Hull.

Elle est née le trente mai mille-neuf-cent-quatre-vingt-onze.
She was born on 30 May 1991.

Il est né le quatorze juin deux-mille-douze.

## Worked example

Write your CV in French.

**Curriculum Vitae**

Jon Smith
22, Main Drive
Newtown
**Tél:** 0044(0) 123 455 678
**Portable:** 0044(0) 87888 990912

**Nationalité:** britannique

**Âge:** 17 ans

**Lieu et date de naissance:** Manchester, 27.09.95
**Éducation:** Granthon High School
**GCSE (brevet):** français, espagnol, maths, anglais, sciences, dessin, religion
**A levels (bac):** maths, technologie, sociologie
**Expérience:** J'ai fait des stages de football et voile. Je travaille une fois par semaine comme moniteur au club des jeunes; je suis le responsable de l'équipe des moins de 13 ans et je les accompagne aux matchs.
**Langues:** J'ai appris le français et l'espagnol à l'école et l'été dernier j'ai passé un mois en Espagne comme serveur. C'était formidable.
**Autres renseignements:** J'ai le permis de conduire depuis deux mois.

- Check you know how to say your **nationality**. Are you **britannique** (British), or more specifically **anglais(e)** (English), **écossais(e)** (Scottish), **gallois(e)** (Welsh), etc.?
- In a CV you cannot avoid lists, but don't go over the top listing absolutely everything. Keep it brief.

### Aiming higher

1. The section to describe your experience gives scope for more complex structures and interesting vocabulary, as well as some past tenses, so make the most of it.

2. The addition of PAST TENSE + OPINION in the languages section of the CV raises the level of the writing. Try to avoid single words, especially when they are identical to English words.

## Now try this

Write your own CV using the model above.

You can use the CV format as the basis of a presentation about yourself or a celebrity, for the speaking assessment.

# Job application

You may meet this job vocabulary in reading and listening extracts.

## Candidature à un poste

| | |
|---|---|
| petite annonce (f) | small ad |
| journal (m) | newspaper |
| lettre (f) | letter |
| agence de voyage (f) | travel agency |
| documentation (f) | information, literature |
| directeur/trice (m/f) | manager |
| gérant(e) (m/f) | manager |
| disponible | available |
| dès début (janvier) | from the start (of January) |
| confiant(e) | confident |
| responsable | responsible |
| travailleur/euse | hard-working |

## Different tenses

If you are writing about yourself, it is all going to be in the first person – but you can use a variety of tenses:

| | | |
|---|---|---|
| PRESENT | je travaille | I work / am working |
| PERFECT | j'ai travaillé | I worked |
| IMPERFECT | je travaillais | I used to work |
| PLUPERFECT | j'avais travaillé | I had worked |
| FUTURE | je travaillerai | I will work |
| CONDITIONAL | je travaillerais | I would work |

L'année dernière, j'ai travaillé à Paris.

## Worked example

READING  target B

Read Emma's letter.

Madame, Monsieur,
J'ai vu votre petite annonce pour le poste de guide touristique dans le journal d'hier et je voudrais poser ma candidature.
J'ai dix-huit ans et je suis anglophone mais j'apprends le français depuis cinq ans et je parle bien l'allemand.
Je suis confiante, responsable et travailleuse et je suis à l'aise avec les adultes.
L'année dernière, j'ai fait un stage de deux semaines dans un agence de voyage.
Je suis disponible pour commencer dès début juin. ...

Don't be distracted by key words appearing in both the answers and the text – here you have **guide touristique** in the letter and 'tourist guide' is mentioned in answer (iii). You have to understand the meaning of the opening paragraph to realise that Emma is applying for a **job** and not writing to a **tourist guide**.

anglophone = native English speaker

Put a cross in the correct box.
Emma is …

(i) applying for a job ☒
(ii) turning down a job offer ☐
(iii) writing to a tourist guide ☐

## Multiple-choice tips

If you really do not have a clue as to the answer in multiple-choice questions, then you will have to guess. Don't waste time agonising – just make a decision and don't leave an answer blank.

## Now try this

READING  target B

Read the letter above and put a cross by the correct answers.

(a) Emma …
  (i) is French.
  (ii) can speak more than one language.
  (iii) doesn't know any German.

(b) Emma …
  (i) is shy.
  (ii) is confident.
  (iii) can't talk easily to adults.

# Job interview

Personal characteristics could well come up in job interviews. As well as the vocabulary on this page, make sure you know the vocabulary on page 3.

## Un entretien

| | |
|---|---|
| chercher | to look for |
| bien s'entendre avec | to get on well with |
| faire du babysitting | to babysit |
| garde d'enfant (f) | childminder |
| qualité (f) | quality |
| ensemble | together |
| calme | calm |
| gentil(le) | kind |
| dès maintenant | straightaway |
| connaissance (f) | knowledge |
| on va vous contacter | we will contact you |

## venir de + infinitive

venir de = to have just done something

Je viens de passer mon bac.
I have just taken my 'bac'.

Tu viens de rentrer.
You have just come back.

Il vient de le dire.
He has just said so.

Nous venons de le faire.
We just did it.

Elle vient de passer un entretien.
She has just had an interview.

---

### Worked example 🎧43 target C

Listen and answer the question **in English**.
What job is the interview for? Childminder

> – Bonjour, vous cherchez un travail comme garde d'enfant?
> – Oui, Madame.

You may not know what **garde d'enfant** means, but if you recognise **enfant** you could have a guess.

### Listening tips

- LOOK at the English questions and try to anticipate the sort of language / phrases you might hear for each one and assess what the text is about.

- You will hear each recording TWICE so don't worry if you don't catch every answer the first time round.

- KEEP PACE with the recording so you don't get stuck worrying about the first question while the recording is moving on to later questions.

- If the pauses between questions seem long, be careful to KEEP CONCENTRATING.

---

### Now try this 🎧44 target C

If the question asks for **two** activities, then you must write two answers. Don't write three.

Listen to the whole interview and answer the questions.

(a) How old is the interviewee?

(b) Has she taken her bac?

(c) What **two** activities does she mention to support her application?

(d) Name **two** of the candidate's characteristics.

(e) How will she be contacted?

# Opinions about jobs

Remember to add plenty of opinions when discussing jobs. Don't forget negative opinions too – they are often used in listening texts.

## Opinions sur les emplois

| C'est ... | It is ... |
|-----------|-----------|
| bien payé | well paid |
| parfait | perfect |
| tranquille | quiet |
| intéressant | interesting |
| facile | easy |
| varié | varied |

| C'est ... | It is ... |
|-----------|-----------|
| mal payé | badly paid |
| bruyant | noisy |
| ennuyeux | boring |
| difficile | difficult |
| fatigant | tiring |
| stressant | stressful |

Les possibilités d'avancement sont bonnes / mauvaises.  The chances of promotion are good / bad.

Il y a trop de responsabilités.  There is too much responsibility.

Les heures sont trop longues.  The hours are too long.

Les heures sont irrégulières / flexibles.  The hours are irregular / flexible.

On est toujours debout / assis(e)(s).  You are always standing / sitting down.

---

### Small words

Listen carefully for small words which completely change the meaning of a sentence, e.g. the negative words ne ... pas.

ce n'est pas amusant = it is not funny

Watch out for these words too:

J'ai peu / beaucoup de responsabilités.  I have little / a lot of responsibility.

J'ai trop de responsabilités.  I have too much responsibility.

---

## Worked example 🎧45 target C

Léna, Noah and Zoë are discussing their jobs. Who says the following?

Léna Noah Zoë

(a) My job is interesting. ☐ ☐ ☐
(b) I am well paid. ☒ ☐ ☐
(c) I have regular hours. ☐ ☐ ☐
(d) I have to stand up all day. ☐ ☐ ☐
(e) I've got no prospects. ☐ ☐ ☐
(f) I don't get paid much. ☐ ☐ ☐

– Selon toi, Léna, c'est un bon métier?
– Ah oui, c'est bien payé, mais ce n'est pas très intéressant.

### Listening tips

- Here, you need to distinguish between different OPINIONS in a listening text. Three people are all using similar vocabulary, but offering different opinions.

- You need to listen to the WHOLE extract before you can answer tasks like these. Listen through once to understand the differences of opinion, and then cross the boxes on a second listening.

- Discriminate between opinions such as Léna saying she is bien payé (well paid) and Noah saying the opposite, mal payé (badly paid).

---

## Now try this 🎧46 target C

Listen to the whole recording and complete the activity above.

# Part-time work

You may discuss part-time jobs – yours or someone else's – in a speaking assessment. Try to use some of the infinitive expressions on this page.

## Un emploi à temps partiel

| | |
|---|---|
| Je remplis les rayons. | I stack shelves. |
| J'ai un job dans un fast-food / une ferme. | I've got a job at a fastfood outlet / farm. |
| Je livre des journaux et des magazines. | I deliver newspapers and magazines. |
| Je fais le ménage. | I do housework. |
| Je travaille dans un centre sportif. | I work in a sports centre. |
| Je lave les voitures des voisins. | I wash neighbours' cars. |
| Je travaille comme plongeur / plongeuse. | I am a washer-up. |
| de temps en temps | from time to time |
| le soir | in the evening |
| le lundi | on Mondays |
| le weekend | at the weekend |
| chaque matin | every morning |
| pendant les vacances | during the holidays |

## Aiming higher

Try to include phrases like these:

**1** POUR + INFINITIVE = IN ORDER TO

Pour gagner de l'argent je fais du babysitting. In order to earn money, I do babysitting.

Il travaille dans le supermarché pour aider son père. He works in the supermarket (in order) to help his dad.

**2** SANS + INFINITIVE = WITHOUT

Sans travailler le weekend, je ne pourrais pas sortir le soir. Without working at the weekend, I wouldn't be able to go out in the evenings.

**3** AVANT DE + INFINITIVE = BEFORE

J'ai trouvé un petit emploi avant d'acheter une voiture. I found a little job before buying a car.

## Worked example

**Tu as un petit job?**

Pour gagner de l'argent, le jeudi soir, je fais du babysitting pour une voisine pendant qu'elle va au cours de yoga. Normalement je n'ai rien à faire parce que le bébé est déjà endormi, ce qui est fantastique parce que je peux regarder la télé avec canal satellite.

**AIMING HIGHER** Non, mais mon grand frère est à l'université et le weekend il travaille dans un supermarché pour gagner de l'argent. Au début il a dû remplir les rayons, puis il a travaillé à la caisse, mais maintenant il est chef de rayon, et ça c'est mieux payé. Il a besoin d'argent parce que l'année prochaine il voudrait bien faire un voyage en train pour visiter toutes les grandes villes d'Europe.

The use of conjunctions, connectives and interesting sentence constructions helps this speech flow – **pendant que** = while, **parce que** = because, **pour gagner de l'argent** = to earn money, **je n'ai rien à faire** = I have nothing to do.

- Talking about someone else and using the **third person** (he / she) adds variety.
- The use of **past** and **future** tenses as well as the present helps to raise the level.
- **il a dû** + infinitive (he had to) is a good way to show that you can use more complex structures.

## Now try this

Talk for one minute about a part-time job you or a member of your family has. Give reasons for why you / they do the job.

- Décris ton petit job.

# Work experience

Work experience is a good topic in which to show off your knowledge of the perfect tense.

## Un stage

J'ai fait mon stage chez un vétérinaire.

| | |
|---|---|
| J'ai passé une semaine dans un bureau. | I spent a week in an office. |
| J'ai lavé des voitures. | I washed cars. |
| J'ai mis des données dans l'ordinateur. | I put data in a computer. |
| J'ai répondu au téléphone. | I answered the phone. |
| J'ai suivi un mécanicien / une secrétaire. | I followed a mechanic / secretary. |
| On m'a donné un uniforme à porter. | I was given a uniform to wear. |
| J'ai travaillé chez un coiffeur / en entreprise. | I worked at a hairdresser's / a firm. |

## Perfect tense: avoir verbs ▸ Page 95

The perfect tense for most verbs is: part of avoir + past participle.

| | |
|---|---|
| j'ai travaillé | I worked |
| il a fait | he did |
| tu as aidé | you helped |
| nous avons nettoyé | we cleaned |
| vous avez mis | you put |
| ils / elles ont répondu | they answered |

J'ai passé quinze jours dans une boulangerie.

NB Remember that aller and other key verbs use être rather than avoir.

## Worked example   LISTENING 47   target C

Solange is talking about her work experience. What does she mention?

Put a cross in the four correct boxes.

A   the other employees ☐
B   her journey to work ☒
C   what she did at lunch time ☐
D   disadvantages of this kind of work ☐
E   what she had to wear ☐
F   what she had to do ☐
G   the days she worked ☐
H   the work she wants to do in the future ☐

– J'ai fait mon stage dans un magasin. C'était en centre-ville donc j'ai dû prendre le métro pour y aller.

## EXAM ALERT!

Most students were able to match **prendre le métro** with answer B, her journey to work, and **un uniforme à porter** with answer E, what she had to wear. Answer D proved the most difficult where students had to match **les heures sont très longues et les clients peuvent être difficiles** with disadvantages of the job.

This was a real exam question that a lot of students struggled with – **be prepared!**   ResultsPlus

## Listening for detail

Listen for as much detail as you can, and, in particular, listen to the grammar, such as a verb tense which might tell you what someone is GOING TO DO rather than what they DO NOW.

## Now try this   LISTENING 48   target C

Listen to the whole recording and complete the activity above.

# My work experience

As well as using the perfect tense to talk about work experience, include a few imperfect phrases such as those on this page.

## Un stage

Le patron / La patronne était sympa.
The boss was nice.

Mes collègues étaient gentils.
My colleagues were kind.

J'étais un peu déçu(e).
I was a bit disappointed.

C'était une expérience positive.
It was a positive experience.

Il n'y avait pas beaucoup à faire.
There was not much to do.

Le travail était bien / mal organisé.
The work was well / badly organised.

Je ne m'entendais pas bien avec les autres.
I didn't get on well with the others.

## Imperfect tense

> Page 97

Use the imperfect tense to describe what things were like generally.

C'était une perte de temps.
It was a waste of time.

Il y avait trop de bruit.
There was too much noise.

J'étais impressionné(e). I was impressed.

Il n'était pas satisfait.
He wasn't satisfied / happy.

On n'avait pas le temps.
We didn't have time.

Je me sentais exploité(e). I felt used.

La patronne n'était pas très sympa.
The boss wasn't very nice.

## Worked example

WRITING

Write about your work experience.

J'ai fait un stage en entreprise où j'ai passé quinze jours dans un bureau. J'ai suivi l'informaticienne et j'ai travaillé sur l'ordinateur. Elle m'a montré comment entrer des données.

**AIMING HIGHER**

J'ai fait trois jours dans un garage où j'ai lavé les voitures. Mes collègues étaient désagréables et je ne m'entendais pas du tout avec eux. J'ai aussi dû faire du café et laver les tasses, ce que je trouvais affreux. Le propriétaire n'avait pas le temps de s'occuper de moi, et je me sentais exploitée. Je ne voudrais pas travailler dans un garage à l'avenir – j'en suis sûre!

Raise your level by linking sentences with the conjunctions **où** (where) and **et** (and). Use pronouns, (e.g. **m'a montré**) to demonstrate a sound knowledge of French grammar. However, there is no opinion here and you could quite easily add **mais je me suis ennuyé** (but I was bored) to improve your answer.

- Include **complex structures** with a wide range of vocabulary and correct agreements.
- Describe your feelings (using a reflexive verb) and also change tense to say what you **had** to do, using **j'ai dû** (I had to).
- Include future plans with a simple conditional **je (ne) voudrais (pas)** + infinitive.

## Now try this

WRITING

Write 200 words about your work experience, including:

- What you did (perfect tense).
- How you felt (imperfect tense).
- What effect it had on your future plans (conditional / future).

# Computers

Some technical language about computers and the internet is listed below. Try to use comparatives wherever you can.

## Les ordinateurs

ordinateur (m)
écran (tactile) (m)
imprimante (f)
touche (f)
clavier (m)
souris (f)

| | |
|---|---|
| effacer | to delete |
| charger | to load |
| copier | to copy / burn |
| mettre en ligne | to upload |
| sauvegarder | to save |
| surfer sur Internet | to surf the internet |
| taper | to type |
| télécharger | to download |
| fichier (m) | file |
| logiciel (m) | software |
| mot de passe (m) | password |
| numérique | digital |
| site Internet / web (m) | website |

### Comparatives
Page 83

Put plus (more), moins (less) and aussi (as) + que around an adjective if you are comparing it with something else.

La souris est plus vieille que l'ordinateur.  The mouse is older than the computer.

Mon ordinateur était moins cher que le tien.  My computer was less expensive than yours.

Je tape aussi vite que toi.
I type as quickly as you.

## Worked example

Answer the question in English.

> Nous avons sélectionné pour vous la meilleure solution pour sauvegarder vos fichiers et les protéger contre les virus, grâce à un logiciel aussi simple qu'efficace ... et en plus, c'est gratuit.

What **two** things does this software claim to do? save files, protect from viruses

## Aiming higher

You need to read for detail in order to give precise answers. Reading for general meaning alone will not be enough to answer the questions correctly.

- You need to locate the words which tell you what the software does, which are **sauvegarder vos fichiers** (save files) and **les protéger contre les virus** (protect them from viruses).
- The question asks for **two** claims, not just one, so make sure you have read the question carefully and answer it completely.

## Now try this

Answer this question in English on the advert above.
- Name **two** more of the software's attributes.

Don't ignore the final adjective **gratuit** – use this if you are struggling to understand the others listed, but do not list all **three**.

# Internet pros and cons

Try to memorise as many of the phrases on this page as you can, so that you'll be able to talk about internet pros and cons.

## Positif et négatif de l'Internet

L'Internet, c'est un moyen pratique de ...
The internet is a good way of ...

  s'informer.

  keeping up-to-date.

  acheter des billets de train / cinéma.

  buying train / cinema tickets.

  rester en contact avec ses amis.

  keeping in touch with friends.

  jouer à des jeux.

  playing games.

L'Internet, c'est dangereux / mauvais quand on...
The internet is dangerous when you ...

  ne surveille pas les enfants.

  don't keep an eye on children.

  passe tout son temps libre devant l'écran.

  spend all your free time in front of a screen.

  donne ses coordonnées sur un forum.

  give your details in a chatroom.

### Opinion phrases

Add an opinion phrase wherever possible to personalise your work.

À mon avis les parents doivent savoir avec qui leurs enfants communiquent en ligne.  In my opinion parents should know who their children are communicating with online.

Selon moi on ne doit pas rester en ligne après huit heures du soir.  According to me you shouldn't stay online after 8pm.

Personnellement je trouve que sur Internet, les livres coûtent moins cher.  Personally, I find that books cost less on the internet.

Les problèmes les plus graves, ce sont les inconvénients techniques.  The biggest problems are technical hitches.

Je fais des recherches pour mes devoirs.
I do research for my homework.

Je fais des achats en ligne.
I do my shopping online.

---

## Worked example 🔊 SPEAKING

Tu aimes utiliser l'Internet?

> J'utilise l'Internet pour faire des recherches pour mes devoirs, pour faire des achats, pour contacter mes amis ... pour tout.

**AIMING HIGHER**
> Selon moi Internet est un moyen rapide d'accéder à toute l'information, mais on ne doit pas oublier les inconvénients. Personnellement je pense que le problème le plus grave, c'est qu'il y a des gens qui harcèlent les autres en ligne. La semaine dernière, on a piraté l'ordinateur de mon frère et un inconnu a fait des achats avec sa carte de crédit. Il dit qu'il ne fera plus d'achats en ligne. Ça, c'est dommage.

Weaknesses in this sample answer are:
- it does not give an opinion
- there is only one tense
- and it simply lists activities.

To give a better answer, you need to:
- use a wide range of appropriate and interesting vocabulary
- use a wide range of structures, including some complex items.
- express and explain a range of ideas and points of view.

il y a des gens qui harcèlent
= there are people who harass

---

## Now try this 🔊 SPEAKING

Talk for one minute about what you think the advantages and disadvantages of the internet are.
- Parle de ce que tu penses de l'Internet.

# Articles 1

Here you will revise how to say 'the', and 'a' or 'some', in French.

## Gender

Every French noun has a gender.
All people, places or things are either masculine (m) or feminine (f).

masculine: le livre (m)    the book
feminine:    la table (f)    the table
The words for 'the' and 'a / some' are:

| | singular | | plural | |
|---|---|---|---|---|
| | masc | fem | masc | fem |
| the | le | la | les | les |
| a / some | un | une | des | des |

le livre    the book    un livre    a book
les livres   the books   des livres   some books

Le and la both become l' if the noun begins with a vowel or silent h:
l'hôpital (m) – hospital
l'église (f) – church

## Plurals

Most French nouns make the plural by adding -s but it is not pronounced.

le chat   the cat   ➡   les chats   the cats
Some nouns add -x in the plural:

* Nouns which end in:

  | -ail | travail | ➡ | travaux | works |
  |---|---|---|---|---|
  | -al | animal | ➡ | animaux | animals |
  | -eau | bureau | ➡ | bureaux | offices |
  | -eu | jeu | ➡ | jeux | games |
  | -ou | bijou | ➡ | bijoux | jewels |

* Nouns ending in -x, -z or -s don't change:

  un os   a bone    deux os   two bones
  un nez   a nose    deux nez   two noses

## Masculine or feminine?

If you don't know the gender of a word, you can look it up in a dictionary or on the internet, but here are some tips:

MASCULINE NOUNS

| male people: | l'homme | the man |
|---|---|---|
| male animals: | le chat | the cat |
| days of the week: | le lundi | Monday |
| months: | juillet | July |
| seasons: | l'été | the summer |

Most nouns which end in:
-age   le village     le garage
-er    le boulanger   baker
-eau   le bureau     office
[except eau (f)   water]

FEMININE NOUNS

female people: la fille    the girl
female animals: la chatte   the female cat
Countries which end in -e: la France
Rivers which end in -e: la Seine
[NB an exception is le Rhône]

Most nouns which end in:
-e    la voiture     the car
-ée   une araignée   spider

All nouns which end in -sion or -tion:
une émission   a programme
la destination   the destination

All nouns ending in -té:
quantité   quantity
identité   identity

## Now try this

**Le**, **la**, **l'** or **les**? Fill in the missing articles.

_____ garçon    _____ mère    _____ étudiants    _____ printemps
_____ Espagne    _____ Loire    _____ condition    _____ bleu
_____ décision    _____ père    _____ garage    _____ plage

Always try to learn the le or la when you learn a new word.

# Articles 2

It is crucial that you can use du, de la, de l' or des to say 'some', and au, à la, à l' or aux to say 'to the'.

## How to say 'some'

| masculine | feminine | beginning with vowel or silent h | plural |
|-----------|----------|-----------------------------------|--------|
| du | de la | de l' | des |

le lait      the milk ➡ du lait      some milk

la confiture   jam     ➡ de la confiture   some jam

l'essence    petrol    ➡ de l'essence   some petrol

les animaux   animals ➡ des animaux    some animals

But after the negative you only use de/d':

Je n'ai pas de pain.    I haven't any bread.

Il n'a pas d'oeufs.
He hasn't any eggs.

- We don't always need to use 'some' in English. Sometimes we miss it out altogether, but you HAVE to use it in French:

  Veux-tu du lait ou du café?
  Do you want milk or coffee?

- And in English, when we ask a question we use 'any':

  Avez-vous des boissons?
  Have you got any drinks?

  Avez-vous du pain?
  Have you got any bread?

## How to say 'to the'

| masculine | feminine | beginning with vowel or silent h | plural |
|-----------|----------|-----------------------------------|--------|
| au | à la | à l' | aux |

au bureau      to the office

à la mairie     to the town hall

à l'école      to (the) school

aux toilettes   to the toilets

On va au collège.

## Now try this

1 How would you tell someone how to go to these places using **aller**? For example, **Allez au carrefour**.
   (a) [..........................] parking (m)
   (b) [..........................] toilettes (pl)
   (c) [..........................] gare (f)
   (d) [..........................] arrêt de bus (m)
   (e) [..........................] feux (pl)
   (f) [..........................] supermarché (m)
   (g) [..........................] château (m)
   (h) [..........................] tour Eiffel (f)

2 Translate these phrases into French.
   (a) I want some bread.
   (b) Have you got any milk?
   (c) He hasn't got any petrol.
   (d) I'm going to school.
   (e) Are you going to the town hall?
   (f) He's going to the toilets.

   You have all the vocabulary you need on the page!

# Adjectives

When using adjectives, you have to think about AGREEMENT and POSITION.

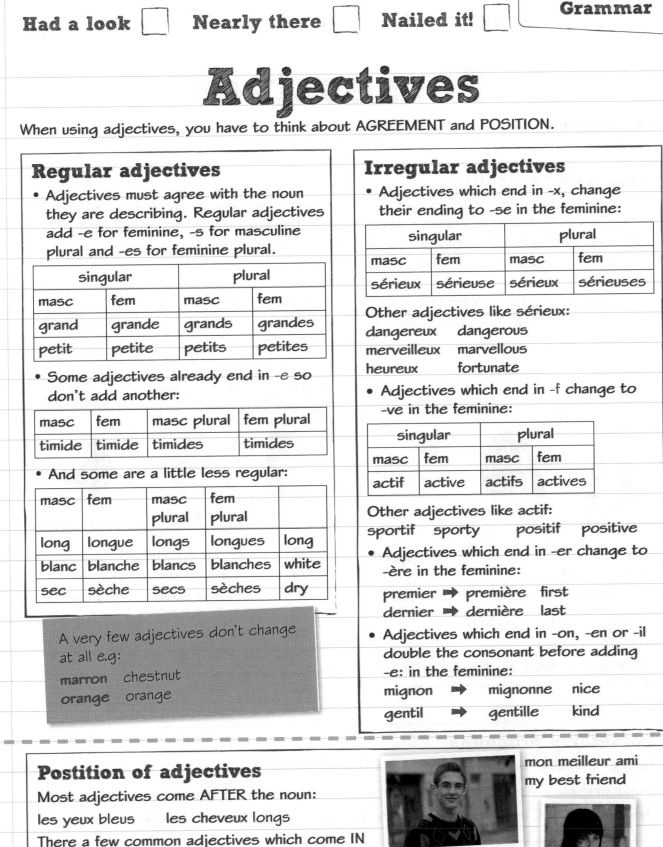

## Regular adjectives

- Adjectives must agree with the noun they are describing. Regular adjectives add -e for feminine, -s for masculine plural and -es for feminine plural.

| singular | | plural | |
|---|---|---|---|
| masc | fem | masc | fem |
| grand | grande | grands | grandes |
| petit | petite | petits | petites |

- Some adjectives already end in -e so don't add another:

| masc | fem | masc plural | fem plural |
|---|---|---|---|
| timide | timide | timides | timides |

- And some are a little less regular:

| masc | fem | masc plural | fem plural | |
|---|---|---|---|---|
| long | longue | longs | longues | long |
| blanc | blanche | blancs | blanches | white |
| sec | sèche | secs | sèches | dry |

A very few adjectives don't change at all e.g:

marron    chestnut
orange    orange

## Irregular adjectives

- Adjectives which end in -x, change their ending to -se in the feminine:

| singular | | plural | |
|---|---|---|---|
| masc | fem | masc | fem |
| sérieux | sérieuse | sérieux | sérieuses |

Other adjectives like sérieux:
dangereux    dangerous
merveilleux    marvellous
heureux    fortunate

- Adjectives which end in -f change to -ve in the feminine:

| singular | | plural | |
|---|---|---|---|
| masc | fem | masc | fem |
| actif | active | actifs | actives |

Other adjectives like actif:
sportif   sporty    positif   positive

- Adjectives which end in -er change to -ère in the feminine:

premier ➡ première   first
dernier ➡ dernière   last

- Adjectives which end in -on, -en or -il double the consonant before adding -e: in the feminine:

mignon ➡ mignonne   nice
gentil ➡ gentille   kind

## Postition of adjectives

Most adjectives come AFTER the noun:

les yeux bleus    les cheveux longs

There a few common adjectives which come IN FRONT OF the noun:

grand(e)   big     vieux / vieille    old
petit(e)   small     nouveau / nouvelle   new
joli(e)   pretty     meilleur(e)      best

mon meilleur ami
my best friend

ma meilleure amie
my best friend

## Now try this

Translate these phrases into French.

1 a little black dog
2 last week
3 My little brother is very active.
4 My best friend (f) is small and shy.
5 Her brother is tall, sporty but a bit serious.

# Possessives

Possessives are used to say 'my', 'your', 'our', etc. They change according to gender and number.

## Possessive adjectives

In French the possessive adjective ('my, 'your', etc.) changes to agree with the GENDER and NUMBER of the noun which follows. There are usually three different words, according to whether the noun is masculine or feminine, singular or plural.

| | |
|---|---|
| ma sœur | my sister (feminine) |
| mon frère | my brother (masculine) |
| mes parents | my parents (plural) |

Remember, son / sa / ses mean both 'his' and 'her'.

> **BE CAREFUL**
> You use mon, ton, son with a feminine noun if it begins with a vowel. For example: mon ami, mon amie – my friend.

| masc | fem | plural | MY |
|---|---|---|---|
| mon | ma | mes | |

| masc | fem | plural | HIS / HER |
|---|---|---|---|
| son | sa | ses | |

| mon jean | ma veste | mes baskets | son pantalon | sa chemise | ses chaussures |

| masc | fem | plural | YOUR |
|---|---|---|---|
| ton | ta | tes | |

ton portable    ta console de jeux    tes jeux

| masc | fem | plural | YOUR |
|---|---|---|---|
| votre | votre | vos | |

votre frère    votre sœur    vos parents

| masc | fem | plural | OUR |
|---|---|---|---|
| notre | notre | nos | |

notre chat    notre chatte    nos chatons

| masc | fem | plural | THEIR |
|---|---|---|---|
| leur | leur | leurs | |

leur garçon    leur fille    leurs enfants

## Possessive pronouns

To say, 'It's mine' or 'They're mine', use the following:

| masc singular | C'est le mien. | masc plural | Ce sont les miens. |
|---|---|---|---|
| fem singular | C'est la mienne. | fem plural | Ce sont les miennes. |

## Now try this

Write these in French.

| | |
|---|---|
| my brother .................................... | her friends (m and f) ............................ |
| his friend (m) ................................. | her mobile.......................................... |
| his friends (m and f) ...................... | my parents .......................................... |
| his bag .......................................... | their friend (m).................................... |
| my sister ........................................ | their friends (m and f) ........................ |
| her friend (f) ................................. | their car ................................ voiture |

# Comparisons

In order to aim for a high grade, you need to be able to use some complex structures such as comparatives and superlatives.

## Comparative

You use the COMPARATIVE when you are comparing two things: my house is BIGGER.

• Form the comparative by putting plus (more) or moins (less) in front of the adjective.

The adjectives have to agree with the noun they are describing.

Mon frère est grand. Simon est plus grand.    My brother is big. Simon is bigger.

Ma sœur est petite. Nathalie est plus petite.    My sister is small. Nathalie is smaller.

To compare two things:

(bigger) than = plus (grand) que:

Nathan est plus grand que Tom.      Nathan is bigger than Tom.

(smaller) than = moins (grand) que:

Ambre est moins grande que sa sœur.    Ambre is smaller than her sister.

as (big) as = aussi (grand) que:

Il est aussi grand que son père.      He is as big as his father.

*Nathan est plus grand que Tom.*

## Superlative

You use the SUPERLATIVE when you are comparing more than two things: my house is THE BIGGEST.

• Form the superlative by adding the definite article le / la / les as well as plus:

le plus grand / la plus grande / les plus grand(e)s    the biggest

le livre le plus intéressant            the most interesting book

la matière la plus ennuyeuse          the most boring subject

---

## Exceptions to the rule

| adjective | comparative | superlative |
|---|---|---|
| bon / bonne   good | meilleur(e)   better | le meilleur / la meilleure   the best |
| mauvais(e)   bad | pire       worse | le / la pire       the worst |

Le film est meilleur que le livre.    The film is better than the book.

le meilleur restaurant    the best restaurant

---

## Now try this

Complete the sentences with the comparative or superlative.

1 L'Everest est la montagne ............................ du monde. [haut] [*highest*]

2 La veste est ............................ que la robe. [+ cher] [*more expensive*]

3 Demain il fera ............................ qu'aujourd'hui. [+ beau] [*nicer*]

4 ............................ solution est de prendre le train. [bon] [*the best*]

5 Julie est ............................ que Fabien. [= intelligent] [*less intelligent*]

6 Le TGV est le train ............................ [rapide]. [*the quickest*]

# Other adjectives

Here you will learn about demonstrative and interrogative adjectives, as well as demonstrative and interrogative pronouns.

Like le, la and les they have to agree with the noun they are referring to.

## Demonstrative adjectives

To say 'this / that', 'these / those':

| masc sing | fem sing | masc plural | fem plural |
|---|---|---|---|
| ce | cette | ces | ces |

ce livre     this / that book

cette fille    this girl

ces livres    these books

ces filles    these girls

You use cet in front of a noun which begins with a vowel or silent h:

cet hôtel    cet espace.

## Interrogative adjectives

To say 'Which?':

| masc sing | fem sing | masc plural | fem plural |
|---|---|---|---|
| quel | quelle | quels | quelles |

Quel enfant?
Which child?
Quelle femme?
Which lady?
Quels garçons?
Which boys?
Quelles filles?
Which girls?

Quelle fille?

## This one, that one

These are pronouns. They replace the noun and answer the question: Which (book)? This one / That ...

| masc sing | fem sing | masc plural | fem plural |
|---|---|---|---|
| celui-ci | celle-ci | ceux-ci | celles-ci |
| celui-là | celle-là | ceux-là | celles-là |

ci means 'here', so celui-ci means 'this one (here)'.

là means 'there', so celui-là means 'that one (there).

## Which one?

These pronouns ask the question 'Which one?': Lequel?

They agree with the noun they represent.

| masc sing | fem sing | masc plural | fem plural |
|---|---|---|---|
| lequel? | laquelle? | lequels? | lesquelles? |

un livre; Lequel?    a book; Which one?
ta jupe; Laquelle?    your skirt; Which one?
les films; Lesquels?    the films; Which ones?
les chaussures; Lesquelles?    the shoes; Which ones?

## Now try this

Fill in the missing words.

**Example:**

Je veux **ce** stylo. – I want this pen.

**Lequel?** – Which one?

**Celui-ci.** – This one.

1 Noé veut .................... veste.
.................... (Which one?)
.................... (This one.)

2 Je préfère .................... portable.
.................... (Which one?)
.................... (That one.)

3 Manon a choisi .................... chaussures.
.................... (Which ones?)
.................... (These ones.)

4 Son frère achète .................... jeux.
.................... (Which ones?)
.................... (Those ones.)

5 On regarde .................... film ce soir?
.................... (Which one?)
.................... (That one.)

# Adverbs

An adverb is a word which 'describes' a verb (hence the name). It tells you HOW an action is done: quickly, slowly, loudly, etc.

## Using and forming adverbs

You use an adverb when you want to bring your work to life, give more detail and explain or describe how something is done.

In English, a lot of adverbs end in -ly.

In French, a lot of adverbs end in -ment.

• You can form adverbs by adding -ment to the feminine form of an adjective.

heureux ➡ heureuse + -ment ➡ heureusement    fortunately

doux ➡ douce + -ment ➡ doucement    quietly

• Some adverbs don't follow this pattern:

vrai ➡ vraiment    really          absolu ➡ absolument    absolutely

## Adverbs of frequency

Other adverbs which tell you how often or when:

| | |
|---|---|
| rarement | rarely |
| d'habitude | usually |
| normalement | normally |
| souvent | often |
| de temps en temps | from time to time |
| régulièrement | regularly |
| quelquefois | sometimes |
| tout de suite | straight away |
| immédiatement | immediately |
| toujours | always |

## Expressions of time

Some adverbs are useful for a time line when narrating a sequence of events:

| | |
|---|---|
| d'abord / au début | at the beginning |
| puis / ensuite / alors | then |
| maintenant | now |
| finalement | finally |
| à l'avenir | in the future |

D'abord j'ai joué au basket puis je suis allé à la piscine.

First of all I played basketball, then I went to the pool.

## Adverbs of position

| | |
|---|---|
| au-dessus | above |
| au-dessous | below |
| dehors | outside |
| dedans | inside |
| derrière | behind |
| en bas | down |
| en haut | up |

## Linking adverbs

| | |
|---|---|
| peut-être | perhaps |
| par conséquent | as a result |
| plutôt | rather |
| probablement | probably |
| alors | so |
| seulement | only |
| en revanche | on the other hand |

## Now try this

Use as many adverbs as you can to make this passage more interesting.

Notre chat a disparu. Il rentre chaque soir vers six heures. J'ai entendu un bruit. J'ai ouvert la porte et j'ai été surpris de voir Max avec trois petit chatons! Il est entré dans la maison. Max n'est plus Max, mais Maxine!

# Object pronouns

You use a pronoun (e.g. it, me, you, them) when you don't want to keep repeating a noun or a name.

Pronouns make your French sound more natural and will help you aim for a higher grade.

## Subject and object

The SUBJECT is the person or thing which is doing the action (verb).

The OBJECT is the person or thing which is having the action (verb) done to it.

| SUBJECT | verb | OBJECT |
|---------|------|--------|
| Tracey | sends | the e-mail. |

| subject | | direct object | | indirect object pronouns | |
|---------|---|---------------|---|--------------------------|---|
| je | I | me | me | me | (to / for) me |
| tu | you | te | you | te | (to / for) you |
| il | he / it | le | him / it | lui | (to / for) him / it |
| elle | she / it | la | her / it | lui | (to / for) her / it |
| nous | we | nous | us | nous | (to / for) us |
| vous | you | vous | you | vous | (to / for) you |
| ils / elles | they | les | them | leur | (to / for) them |

## Direct object pronouns

In French, the object pronoun comes in front of the verb.

| I send it. | Je l'envoie. |
|------------|--------------|
| He does it. | Il le fait. |
| We buy them. | Nous les achetons. |
| They invite us. | Ils nous invitent. |

In French, the object pronoun 'it' or 'them' is the same as the word for 'the'.

## Word order

• In a negative sentence, the pronoun goes after the ne:

Tu ne la regardes pas?
Aren't you watching it?

• In the perfect tense, the pronoun comes in front of the AUXILIARY verb (avoir or être):

Je l'ai déjà regardé(e).   I have already seen it.

Nous les avons acheté(e)s.   We bought them.

The past participle agrees with the object pronoun, so if the object is feminine or plural the past participle must agree.

## Indirect object pronouns

You use the indirect object pronoun to replace a noun that has à in front of it.

Sarah envoie un texto à son ami.
Sarah is sending a text to her boyfriend.

Elle lui envoie un texto.
She is sending him a text.

When you have le / la / les and lui / leur in the same sentence, the le / la / les come first:

Elle la lui envoie.   She sends it to him.
Je le leur ai donné.   I gave it to them.

## Now try this

Rewrite the sentences, replacing the object of each sentence with a pronoun.

1 Il a envoyé un message.
2 Je n'ai pas regardé l'émission.
3 Il n'a pas acheté les chaussures.
4 Tu as vu ce film?
5 Sarah a lu ce livre.
6 Mes parents ont acheté une voiture.

# More pronouns: *y* and *en*

Use y and en in your writing and speaking to demonstrate that you can use a wide range of structures.

---

## *y* there

- You use y to refer to a place which has already been mentioned, for example en ville, à la gare.

  Tu vas à la gare? Oui, j'y vais.    Are you going to the station? Yes, I'm going there.

- It is not always translated in English, but you have to include it in French.

  Vous allez en ville? Oui, nous y allons.    Are you going to town? Yes we're going there.

  J'aime aller à Paris. Moi aussi, j'aime y aller.    I like going to Paris. Me too, I like going there.

- You also use it with verbs which take à:

  Tu joues au football? Oui, j'y joue.

  Do you play football? Yes I play it.

- y is also used in some common phrases:

  il y a   there is / there are         Vas-y!   Go on!

  Il y a beaucoup à faire.   There is a lot to do.    Allons-y!   Let's go!

---

## *en* of it / of them

- You use en to replace a noun or *du / de la / de l' / des* + noun which has already been mentioned.

  Tu veux du café? Oui, j'en veux bien.
  Do you want some coffee? Yes, I'd like some.

- It is not always translated in English, but you have to include it in French.

  Tu manges de la viande? Oui, j'en mange beaucoup.
  Do you eat meat? Yes, I eat a lot (of it).

- en is also used with expressions of quantity:

  Tu as combien de frères? J'en ai deux.    How many brothers have you got? I've got two (of them).

  Tu as acheté des pommes? Oui, j'en ai acheté un kilo.
  Did you buy some apples? Yes, I brought a kilo (of them).

- en is also used in the following common phrases:

  Qu'est-ce que tu en penses?   What do you think of it?
  J'en ai marre.    I'm fed up.
  Je m'en vais.    I'm going.

---

## Now try this

Rewrite the sentences, replacing the nouns with **y** or **en**.

1 Je suis déjà allé au cinéma.
2 J'ai déjà mangé trop de chips.
3 Je suis allé à Paris hier.
4 Je vais au cinéma de temps en temps.
5 On va souvent au supermarché.
6 Je ne mange jamais de frites.

# Other pronouns

Use the pronouns qui, que, où and dont in your writing and speaking to show that you can use a wide range of structures.

## Relative pronouns qui and que

These are pronouns which relate back to something or someone you have just mentioned:

- Qui (who / which) replaces the SUBJECT of the sentence. You know this, as you have been using it from the start:

  J'ai un frère qui s'appelle John.
  I have a brother who is called John.

  Ma sœur est la fille qui porte une robe bleue.
  My sister is the girl who is wearing a blue dress.

- Que (whom / which) replaces the OBJECT of a sentence:

  L'homme que j'ai vu ne portait pas de lunettes.
  The man (whom) I saw didn't wear glasses.

  J'ai acheté le pantalon que j'ai trouvé sur l'Internet.
  I bought the trousers which I found on the internet.

  C'était la même personne que j'avais vue en ville.
  It was the same person that I had seen in town.

## More pronouns: où and dont

- Où (where) refers back to a place that has been mentioned previously or is known:

  L'endroit où j'ai trouvé mon porte-monnaie est loin d'ici.
  The place where I found my purse is far away.

  La maison où il habite est très grande.
  The house where he lives is very big.

la maison
où j'habite

- Dont means 'whose / of'; 'whom / about whom':

  Le monsieur dont j'ai trouvé les lunettes …
  The man whose glasses I found …

  La fille dont on a déjà parlé …
  The girl whom we have already talked about …

  Le film dont j'ai vu la bande-annonce …
  The film whose trailer I saw …

C'est le garçon
dont j'ai parlé.

## Now try this

Complete these sentences with **qui**, **que**, **où** or **dont**.

1 Mon ami .......................................... s'appelle Bruno est fana de football.
2 L'émission .......................................... j'ai vue hier n'était pas passionnante.
3 Le quartier .......................................... ils habitent est vraiment calme.
4 Le prof .......................................... je vous ai déjà parlé.
5 Elle a une sœur .......................................... est prof.
6 J'ai accepté le stage .......................................... mon prof m'a proposé.

# Present tense: -ER verbs

Good news! Most French verbs are -er verbs, and most -er verbs are regular.

## Forming the present tense of -er verbs

The endings are:

| je | -e | nous | -ons |
|---|---|---|---|
| tu | -es | vous | -ez |
| il / elle | -e | ils / elles | -ent |

JOUER   TO PLAY

| I play | je joue | we play | nous jouons |
|---|---|---|---|
| you play | tu joues | you play | vous jouez |
| he / she / one plays | il / elle / on joue | they play | ils / elles jouent |

New verbs describing actions connected with technology are all -er verbs:

télécharger (to download)
tchater (to chat)
bloguer (to blog)

## Some common -er verbs

| aimer | to like | donner | to give | quitter | to leave |
|---|---|---|---|---|---|
| aider | to help | écouter | to listen | rester | to stay |
| arriver | to arrive | entrer | to enter | téléphoner | to telephone |
| bavarder | to chat | habiter | to live | travailler | to work |
| décider | to decide | manger | to eat | trouver | to find |
| détester | to hate | penser | to think | visiter | to visit |

Some -er verbs have spelling changes. These are usually to make them easier to pronounce:

- Verbs which end in -ger in the infinitive: manger, nager, plonger
  add -e in the nous form: nous mangeons to keep the 'g' sound soft.

- Verbs which end in -ler and -ter in the infinitive: appeler and rappeler
  double the l or t in the singular je, tu, il / elle / on and in the third person plural:
  je m'appelle, je jette.

- Verbs which end in -yer in the infinitive: payer and envoyer
  change the y to i in the singular je, tu, il / elle / on and in the third person plural:
  j'envoie, elle paie.

- Some verbs change e or é to è, for example acheter ➡ j'achète; se lever ➡ je me lève
  préférer ➡ je préfère. The change occurs in the je, tu, il / elle / on and ils / elles forms
  but the nous and vous forms revert to the stem:

| je préfère | nous préférons |
|---|---|
| tu préfères | vous préférez |
| il / elle / on préfère | ils / elles préfèrent |

## Now try this

Complete the passage with the correct parts of the verbs in brackets.

Je (s'appeler) Lou. J'ai une sœur qui (s'appeler) Marina et qui (jouer) au tennis. Je (préférer) faire de la danse. Je (chanter) et je (jouer) de la guitare. Le soir nous (rentrer) à cinq heures et nous (manger) un casse-croûte. Puis je (tchater) avec mes amis, et j'(écouter) de la musique. Quelquefois mon frère et moi* (jouer) aux jeux vidéo ou (télécharger) un film pour regarder plus tard.

* mon frère et moi = we! Which form are you going to use?

# -IR and -RE verbs

There are two groups of -ir verbs: those which take -ss in the plural forms and those which don't.

## -ir verbs which take -ss

**FINIR   TO FINISH**

| je | finis | nous finissons |
|---|---|---|
| tu | finis | vous finissez |
| il / elle / on | finit | ils / elles finissent |

Verbs like finir:

choisir   to choose

By now you will have noticed that the je, tu and il / elle forms of most verbs sound the same BUT they are not all spelled the same, so be careful when you are writing!

## -ir verbs which don't take -ss

**PARTIR   TO LEAVE**

| je pars | nous partons |
|---|---|
| tu pars | vous partez |
| il / elle / on part | ils / elles partent |

Verbs like partir:

dormir   to sleep (je dors)

sortir    to go out (je sors)

-ir verbs are sometimes referred to as -s -s -t verbs. Can you think of a reason why?

## -re verbs

**RÉPONDRE   TO REPLY**

| je réponds | nous répondons |
|---|---|
| tu réponds | vous répondez |
| il / elle / on répond | ils / elles répondent |

Verbs like répondre:

| attendre | to wait |
|---|---|
| vendre | to sell |
| entendre | to hear |
| perdre | to lose |
| descendre | to go down |

## Irregular -re verbs

**DIRE   TO SAY**

| je dis | nous disons |
|---|---|
| tu dis | vous dites |
| il / elle / on dit | ils / elles disent |

Verbs like dire:

| lire | to read | BUT nous lisons, vous lisez |
|---|---|---|
| écrire | to write | BUT écrivons, écrivez, écrivent |
| boire | to drink | BUT buvons, buvez, boivent |

prendre (to take), comprendre (to understand) and apprendre (to learn) are regular except for the nous, vous and ils / elles forms:

| je prends | nous prenons |
|---|---|
| tu prends | vous prenez |
| il / elle / on prend | ils / elles prennent |

## Now try this

Complete these sentences with the correct part of the verb in brackets.

1 Le matin je (sortir) à sept heures et demie.
2 Le mardi les cours (finir) à cinq heures.
3 Mon copain et moi ne (boire) pas de coca.
4 Le train (partir) à 8h20.
5 Nous (apprendre) l'espagnol.
6 Pendant les vacances, nous (dormir) sous la tente.
7 Mes copains (choisir) des frites.

Je dors sous la tente.

# avoir and être

TO HAVE (avoir) and TO BE (être) are two of the most common verbs used in French. They are both IRREGULAR, so you need to learn their different parts really carefully.

## avoir

| | |
|---|---|
| j'ai | I have |
| tu as | you have (informal) |
| il a | he has |
| nous avons | we have |
| vous avez | you have (formal) |
| ils ont | they have |

### When to use avoir

In French you use avoir to describe your age, or to say that you HAVE hunger or fear or cold.

| | |
|---|---|
| J'ai seize ans. | I am 16 years old. |
| J'ai faim. | I am hungry. |
| Il a peur des fantômes. | He is afraid of ghosts. |
| J'ai froid. | I am cold. |

## être

| | |
|---|---|
| Je suis | I am |
| tu es | you are (informal) |
| il est | he is |
| nous sommes | we are |
| vous êtes | you are (formal) |
| ils sont | they are |

The most common mistake with être is to add it when you are using other verbs. Don't just replace 'am' with suis.

| | |
|---|---|
| je parle | I am talking |
| nous allons | we are going |

## Useful phrases with avoir and être

| | |
|---|---|
| J'ai trois frères. | I have three brothers. |
| Vous avez tort. | You're wrong. |
| J'ai mal à la tête. | I have a headache. |
| J'ai besoin d'un stylo. | I need a pen. |
| Je suis anglais(e). | I am English. |
| La table est marron. | The table is brown. |
| Nous sommes frères. | We are brothers. |
| Ils sont etudiants. | They are students. |

## Auxiliary verbs

Avoir and être are both used as AUXILIARY VERBS. This means they are used to make other TENSES. You can use the present tense of avoir and être to make the perfect tense. Don't forget to make agreements with être.

| | |
|---|---|
| J'ai mangé. | I have eaten. |
| Nous avons payé. | We have paid. |
| Je suis allé(e). | I have gone (or I went). |
| Il est parti. | He has left. |

## Now try this

1 Complete this passage. All the missing words are parts of the verb **avoir**.

Nous .......... un petit chaton. Il est tout noir mais il .......... les yeux verts. Il .......... toujours faim. Il .......... beaucoup de jouets mais j'.......... une balle de ping pong qu'il adore et mon petit frère .......... un petit oiseau en fourrure qu'il dechire. .......... -tu un animal?

2 Complete this passage. All the missing words are parts of the verb **être**.

Je .......... britannique. Je .......... né en Angleterre. Mes parents .......... italiens. Ils .......... nés en Italie mais ils habitent ici depuis vingt ans. Mon frère .......... sportif. Il .......... champion régional de judo. Ma soeur .......... paresseuse. En revanche je .......... charmant!

You can replace mes parents with ils and the sentence still makes sense. So the right part of the verb here is mes parents sont.

# aller and faire

Aller and faire are two of the most important verbs, and guess what? They are both irregular!

## aller   to go

| | |
|---|---|
| je vais | nous allons |
| tu vas | vous allez |
| il / elle / on va | ils / elles vont |

Je vais à la piscine.

## faire   to do

| | |
|---|---|
| je fais | nous faisons |
| tu fais | vous faites |
| il / elle / on fait | ils / elles font |

Did you notice the pattern?

The ils / elles form:

aller ➡ vont; faire ➡ font; avoir ➡ ont; être ➡ sont

## Using aller

Aller is a very common verb. Use it to say where you and your friends go:

Je vais au collège à huit heures.
I go to school at 8 o'clock.

Elise va à la patinoire.
Élise is going to the skating rink.

Mon frère va au cinéma.
My brother goes to the cinema.

Samedi on va au stade.
On Saturdays we go to the stadium.

Le dimanche vous allez à l'église.
On Sundays you go to church.

Le weekend ils vont en ville.
At the weekend, they go into town.

## Using faire

Faire is used in lots of expressions, especially for talking about the weather:

| | |
|---|---|
| Il fait beau. | It is fine. |
| Il fait du vent. | It is windy. |
| Il fait du soleil. | It is sunny. |

It is also used for talking about activities:

Je fais de la natation / de la danse / du VTT.
I do swimming / dancing / mountain biking.

Je fais de l'équitation.

## Now try this

1 Complete the sentences with the correct parts of **aller**, then translate them into English.
 (a) Je ........................... au collège à huit heures.
 (b) Nous y ........................... en car de ramassage.
 (c) Le soir, on ........................... au centre de sports.
 (d) Ma sœur ........................... à la piscine et moi, je ........................... au gymnase.
 (e) Mes parents ........................... au bar, avec les autres parents!

2 Complete this passage with the correct parts of **faire**, then translate it into English.
 En hiver je ................... du ski. Mon frère ................... du surf et mes parents ................... aussi du ski.  Ma sœur ne ................... pas de ski mais nous ................... du patinage ensemble. Que ...................-vous?

# Modal verbs

Modals are verbs which are used together with the infinitive of another verb:
pouvoir (can), vouloir (want to), devoir (have to) and savoir (know how to).

## pouvoir to be able to

| je peux | nous pouvons |
|---|---|
| tu peux | vous pouvez |
| il / elle / on peut | ils / elles peuvent |

Je peux aller au cinéma.
I can go to the cinema.

## vouloir to want to

| je veux | nous voulons |
|---|---|
| tu veux | vous voulez |
| il / elle / on veut | ils / elles veulent |

Je veux manger à la pizzeria.
I want to eat at the pizzeria.

## devoir to have to

| je dois | nous devons |
|---|---|
| tu dois | vous devez |
| il / elle / on doit | ils / elles doivent |

Je dois être à l'heure.
I have to be on time.

## savoir to know how to

| je sais | nous savons |
|---|---|
| tu sais | vous savez |
| il / elle / on sait | ils / elles savent |

Je sais faire du ski.
I know how to ski.

## Now try this

1  **Je veux y aller mais je ne peux pas.**
   Complete these sentences in French using the example above and changing the verbs and pronoun to match the subjects.
   **(a)** Martin ...................................................................
   ........................................................................................
   **(b)** Nous ......................................................................
   ........................................................................................
   **(c)** Vous ......................................................................
   ........................................................................................
   **(d)** Mes parents .........................................................
   ........................................................................................

2  Write these sentences in French.
   **(a)** I have to do my homework.
   **(b)** I don't know how to do the maths.
   **(c)** Do you know how to do the French?
   **(d)** We have to learn the verbs.
   **(e)** My French friends have to write an essay. [une dissertation]
   **(f)** I don't have to write an essay – I just have to answer the questions.

> Common mistakes are:
> 1 Forgetting that **peux** and **veux** become **peut** and **veut** in the third person, including after **on**.
> 2 Forgetting that **dois** and **sais** become **doit** and **sait** in the third person. The third person **never** ends in -s.

# Reflexive verbs

A reflexive verb is a verb used with an extra little pronoun, for example s'appeler (to be called).

## Reflexives and their pronouns

To talk about doing something to yourself, you use a reflexive verb. These verbs need a pronoun which comes between the subject and the verb.

laver – to wash (the car) ➡ se laver – to get washed

lever – to raise (hand, finger, feet) ➡ se lever – to get up

Reflexive pronouns:  je + me          nous + nous
                     tu + te          vous + vous
                     il / elle / on + se   ils / elles + se

---

## The verb s'appeler

appeler     to call

s'appeler   to call yourself / be called

je m'appelle
tu t'appelles
il / elle / on s'appelle
nous nous appelons
vous vous appelez
ils / elles s'appellent

## The verb se laver

laver       to wash

se laver    to get washed (wash yourself)

je me lave
tu te laves
il / elle / on se lave
nous nous lavons
vous vous lavez
ils / elles se lavent

---

## Common reflexive verbs

There are lots of interesting reflexive verbs. The following are useful ones to learn:

s'ennuyer      to get bored je m'ennuie

s'étonner      to be surprised je m'étonne

s'endormir     to fall asleep je m'endors

se reposer     to rest je me repose

se coucher     to go to bed je me couche

se promener    to go for a walk je me promène

se bronzer     to sunbathe je me bronze

## Perfect tense

In the perfect tense all reflexive verbs take être. So the past participle must AGREE with the subject:

Je me suis lavé(e).   I got washed.

Il s'est promené tout seul.
He went for a walk on his own.

Nous nous sommes vite habillé(e)s.
We got dressed quickly.

Vous vous êtes levé(e)(s) trop tard.
You got up too late.

Tu t'es couché(e) de bonne heure?
Did you go to bed early?

Mes parents se sont disputés.
My parents argued.

---

## Now try this

Complete the sentences in this passage with the correct form of the reflexive verb in brackets.

Je ne (s'entendre) pas bien avec mon grand frère. Il (se moquer) de moi. Nous (se disputer) souvent. Je (s'entendre) mieux avec ma sœur. On (s'amuser) bien ensemble. Nous (se coucher) de bonne heure parce que le matin nous (se lever) à six heures – nous, c'est-à-dire toute la famille sauf mon frère qui ne (se réveiller) pas. Quand finalement il (se lever), il ne (se doucher) pas parce qu'il n'a pas le temps.

# The perfect tense 1

The perfect tense is one of the tenses you use to talk about the past. It is called the passé composé in French. Many verbs use avoir to form the perfect tense.

## Formation

The perfect tense of MOST verbs is made up of the verb TO HAVE (avoir) and the PAST PARTICIPLE.

| j'ai | nous avons |
| tu as | vous avez + past participle |
| il / elle / on a | ils / elles ont |

J'ai joué au tennis.
I have played tennis / I played tennis.

## Use of the perfect tense

You use the perfect tense when you are talking about something that happened at a specific time in the past:

Hier soir j'ai regardé un film.
Last night I watched a film.

L'année dernière, mes parents ont acheté une voiture.
Last year my parents bought a car.

## Forming the past participle

For -er verbs, take off the -er and add –é:

manger ➡ mangé
regarder ➡ regardé

J'ai mangé
une crêpe.

For –ir verbs, take off the -r:

finir ➡ fini
dormir ➡ dormi

For -re verbs, take off the -re and add -u:

répondre ➡ répondu
attendre ➡ attendu

There are quite a lot of IRREGULAR past participles and they are the verbs you probably need most – you simply need to learn them.

| avoir ➡ eu | savoir ➡ su |
| être ➡ été | faire ➡ fait |
| mettre ➡ mis | dire ➡ dit |
| voir ➡ vu | écrire ➡ écrit |
| lire ➡ lu | boire ➡ bu |
| vouloir ➡ voulu | prendre ➡ pris |
| devoir ➡ dû | comprendre ➡ compris |
| pouvoir ➡ pu | |

## Negative sentences

In a negative sentence, you put the ne ... pas round the part of avoir:

Je n'ai pas vu le film.
I haven't seen the film.

Il n'a pas joué au foot.
He did not play football.

## Useful phrases

Use these with the perfect tense:

| samedi dernier | last Saturday |
| la semaine dernière | last week |
| le weekend dernier | last weekend |
| hier | yesterday |

## Now try this

Put the infinitives in brackets into the perfect tense to complete the text.

Mercredi dernier j' (prendre) le bus pour aller en ville. J'y (rencontrer) un ami. Nous (faire) les magasins. J'(vouloir) acheter des baskets rouges mais elles étaient trop chères. Nous (manger) des burgers et comme boisson j' (choisir) un coca. Mon copain (boire) un milkshake fraise. J' (laisser) mon sac au bar. Je devais y retourner mais par conséquent j' (rater) le bus et j' (devoir) rentrer à pied.

# The perfect tense 2

Most verbs form the perfect tense with avoir BUT some verbs use être instead. They are mostly verbs to do with movement.

## Verbs which take être

The following 14 verbs take être + the past participle in the perfect tense:

| | |
|---|---|
| aller / venir | to go / to come |
| arriver / partir | to arrive / to depart |
| entrer / sortir | to enter / to leave |
| monter / descendre | to go up / to go down |
| rester / tomber | to stay / to fall |
| naître / mourir | to be born / to die |
| rentrer / revenir | to return |

ALL reflexive verbs also take être.

MRS VAN DER TRAMP spells out the first letters of the 14 verbs listed above and may be useful in helping you to remember them!

## Formation

| ÊTRE: | + | PAST PARTICIPLES: |
|---|---|---|
| je suis | | allé / venu |
| tu es | | arrivé / parti |
| il / elle / on est | | entré / sorti |
| nous sommes | | monté / descendu |
| vous êtes | | né / mort |
| ils / elles sont | | rentré / revenu |

Note how the past participle changes according to who is doing the action:

| | |
|---|---|
| Je suis allé(e). | I went. |
| Elle est arrivé(e). | She arrived. |
| Nous sommes monté(e)(s). | We climbed. |
| Ils sont parti(s). | They left. |

## Agreement of the past participle

With verbs which take être, the past participle agrees with the subject of the verb (a bit like adjectives):

Je suis allé(e)
Tu es allé(e)
Il est allé
Elle est allée
Nous sommes allé(e)s
Vous êtes allé(e)(s)
Ils sont allés
Elles sont allées

## Aiming higher

- You should be able to use the perfect tense if you are aiming at a higher grade.
- Remember, you use the perfect tense when you are talking about one specific time in the past, so you are likely to start the sentence with a time expression referring to the past.
For example:

Samedi dernier ...
Hier ...
Hier soir ...
Il y a deux jours ...
Pendant les vacances ...

## Now try this

Put the infinitives in brackets into the perfect tense to complete the sentences.

1 Samedi dernier je (se lever) de bonne heure.
2 Le matin je (aller) jouer au football.
3 Je (sortir) à dix heures.
4 L'autre équipe (ne pas venir).
5 Nous y (rester) une heure, puis nous (rentrer).
6 Je (arriver) à la maison juste avant midi.

Je suis allé(e) au match.

# The imperfect tense

The imperfect is another verb tense you use to talk about the past.

## Forming the imperfect

First, take the nous form of the present tense and remove the -ons ending:

nous habit~~ons~~

Then add the following imperfect endings:

| | |
|---|---|
| je -ais | nous -ions |
| tu -ais | vous -iez |
| il / elle / on -ait | ils / elles -aient |

**HABITER TO LIVE**

| | |
|---|---|
| j'habitais | nous habitions |
| tu habitais | vous habitiez |
| il / elle / on habitait | ils / elles habitaient |

> Good news: all verbs except être are regular in the imperfect tense.

## Using the imperfect

You use the imperfect tense to describe:

1 What WAS HAPPENING:
   Il pleuvait.  It was raining.

2 What USED TO happen:
   Quand j'étais jeune, je jouais au foot. When I was young, I used to play football.

3 What was ONGOING when something else happened:
   Je regardais la television, lorsque quelqu'un a sonné.  I was watching TV when someone rang.

> The key words to look out for are: 'was / were ...ing' and 'used to ...'.

## Some common verbs

These are a few common verbs you should be able to use in the imperfect.

| Present | Imperfect | English |
|---|---|---|
| voul/ons | je voul+ais | I wanted |
| av/ons | j'av+ais | I had |
| all/ons | j'all+ais | I was going |
| buv/ons | je buv+ais | I was drinking |
| mange/ons | je mange+ais | I was eating |
| achet/ons | j'achet+ais | I was buying |
| finiss/ons | je finiss+ais | I was finishing |
| dorm/ons | je dorm+ais | I was sleeping |

## être in the imperfect

The only IRREGULAR verb in the imperfect tense is être. The stem is ét- and you add the normal imperfect endings to this stem:

| | |
|---|---|
| j'étais | I was |
| tu étais | you were |
| il / elle / on était | he / she was |
| nous étions | we were |
| vous étiez | you were |
| ils / elles étaient | they were |

**Now try this**

Complete the text with the imperfect tense of the verbs in the box, then translate it into English.

Why is it written in the imperfect tense?

Quand j'......................................jeune j'......................................à la campagne. Nous ...................................... un grand jardin où je ...................................... au foot avec mes frères. Le samedi on ...................................... au marché en ville. Il y ...................................... beaucoup de vendeurs de fruits et légumes et un kiosque à journaux où j'...................................... des bonbons. Nous ........... des merguez (des saucisses épicées) et nous ...................................... du coca. On ...................................... en bus avec tous nos voisins et nos achats!

| avoir être habiter jouer aller acheter manger boire rentrer |
|---|

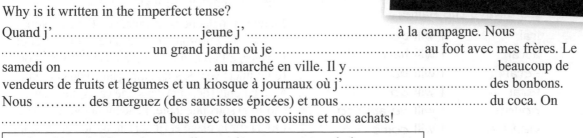

# The future tense

To aim for a high grade you need to use the future tense as well as the present and past!

## Near future tense

When you are talking about what you are GOING to do, use the verb to go (aller) + an infinitive, just as in English:

Je vais aller …   I am going to go …

Ils vont jouer au tennis.
They are going to play tennis.

Mon copain va rentrer à 21h00.   My friend is going to go home at 9 o'clock.

On va se retrouver en ville.
We are going to meet in town.

Remember all the parts of aller (to go):

| je vais | nous allons | |
|---------|-------------|------------|
| tu vas | vous allez | + infinitive |
| il / elle / on va | ils / elles vont | |

Remember, the INFINITIVE is the part of the verb you will find in the dictionary – usually ending in -er, -ir or -re.
For example:
-er: jouer / manger
-ir: finir / choisir / sortir
-re: lire / dire

## Future tense

If you are aiming for a top grade, you will need to be able to understand and use the 'proper' future. It is used to say what you WILL do.

The future is made from the INFINITIVE + FUTURE TENSE ENDINGS:

| -er verbs | manger | ➡ je mangerai | I will eat |
| -ir verbs | finir | ➡ je finirai | I will finish |
| -re verbs | répondre | ➡ je répondrai | I will reply |

The future ENDINGS are the same as the present tense of avoir except for the nous and vous forms:

| je mangerai | nous mangerons |
|-------------|----------------|
| tu mangeras | vous mangerez |
| il / elle / on mangera | ils / elles mangeront |

## Which future to use?

NEAR FUTURE (futur proche):
I AM GOING TO PLAY football tonight.
This is a simple fact.

PROPER FUTURE (futur):
I WILL PLAY football tonight.

You might be:
• expressing an intention.
• responding to a suggestion that you might not do something.

Je jouerai au babyfoot au café.

## Irregular verbs

BE CAREFUL! There are a few common verbs which don't use the infinitive, but have an irregular stem. The good news is the endings are always the same.

| aller | irai | I will go |
| avoir | aurai | I will have |
| être | serai | I will be |
| faire | ferai | I will do |
| pouvoir | pourrai | I will be able to |
| venir | viendrai | I will come |
| voir | verrai | I will see |
| vouloir | voudrai | I will want |

### Now try this

Put all the infinitives in brackets into the future tense to complete the text.

L'année prochaine nous (aller) en France. Nous (prendre) l'Eurostar. On (partir) de Londres et on (arriver) à Paris. Puis on (changer) de train et on (continuer) vers le sud. Nous (faire) du camping. Mes parents (dormir) dans une caravane mais je (dormir) sous une tente. Pendant la journée nous (aller) sur la plage et (jouer) au basket et au tennis. Le soir on (manger) au resto. On (se faire) des amis.

# The conditional

You should know a few verbs in the conditional and be able to use them in your writing and speaking in order to aim for a higher mark.

## The conditional

The conditional is used to say what you WOULD do:

je voudrais – I would like
je jouerais – I would play

It is also used for making suggestions:

on pourrait ... – we could ...

The conditional is formed in a similar way to the future. It uses the same stem (usually the infinitive) but then adds the same endings as the imperfect tense:

manger ➡ je mangerais  I would eat

finir    ➡ je finirais     I would finish

vendre ➡ je vendrais    I would sell

You may meet the conditional after si (if):

Si + imperfect tense + conditional

Si tu mangeais correctement, tu n'aurais plus faim.

If you ate properly you wouldn't be hungry.

## Irregular conditionals

Irregular conditionals use the same stems as the the irregular future:

| Infinitive | Conditional | English |
|---|---|---|
| aller | j'irais | I would go |
| avoir | j'aurais | I would have |
| être | je serais | I would be |
| faire | je ferais | I would do |
| pouvoir | je pourrais | I would be able to |
| venir | je viendrais | I would come |
| voir | je verrais | I would see |
| vouloir | je voudrais | I would like |

The endings are always the same:

je mangerais            nous mangerions
tu mangerais            vous mangeriez
il / elle mangerait     ils / elles mangeraient

Je voudrais aller au concert ce soir.
I'd like to go to the concert this evening.

On pourrait faire du bowling?
We could go bowling?

## Now try this

Put the infinitives in the following sentences in the conditional.

1 Je (vouloir) aller en Italie.

2 Si j'avais assez d'argent, j'(aller) en Inde.

3 Nous (pouvoir) faire un long voyage.

4 Tu (aimer) voir ce film?

5 Je (préférer) manger au restaurant.

6 Si j'avais faim, je (manger) une pizza.

7 Il (vouloir) aller en ville samedi.

8 On (pouvoir) aller à la patinoire cet après-midi?

9 Tu (voir) le match si tu restais encore deux jours.

10 Vous (vouloir) quelque chose à boire?

Had a look ☐    Nearly there ☐    Nailed it! ☐

# The pluperfect tense

The pluperfect is another past tense; you don't have to USE it at GCSE but you should be able to RECOGNISE it. It is used to say what you HAD done.

## The pluperfect tense

You use the pluperfect to talk about an event that took place one step further back than another past event.

Whereas the perfect tense means 'I did something' or 'I have done something', the pluperfect is used to say what you HAD done.

We HAD finished dinner (pluperfect) when she knocked on the door. (perfect)

J'avais déjà mangé quand je suis allé au cinéma.
I had already eaten when I went to the cinema.

## How does it work?

The pluperfect is formed like the perfect tense with the auxiliary (avoir or être) + the past participle.

The difference is that it uses the IMPERFECT of the auxiliary:

J'avais déjà mangé.     I had already eaten.

J'étais allé(e) en ville.  I had gone into town.

The verbs which take être are the same ones which take être in the perfect tense (see page 96). Remember MRS VAN DER TRAMP.

Also remember that the past participle of être verbs must agree with the subject.

Mes parents étaient partis en vacances et j'étais seul à la maison.
My parents had gone on holiday and I was alone in the house.

## The pluperfect with avoir

Here is an avoir verb in the pluperfect:

| | |
|---|---|
| j'avais mangé | I had eaten |
| tu avais mangé | you had eaten |
| il / elle / on avait mangé | he / she / one had eaten |
| nous avions mangé | we had eaten |
| vous aviez mangé | you had eaten |
| ils / elles avaient mangé | they had eaten |

## The pluperfect with être

Here is an être verb in the pluperfect:

| | |
|---|---|
| j'étais allé(e) | I had gone |
| tu étais allé(e) | you had gone |
| il / on était allé | he / one had gone |
| elle / on était allé(e) | she / one had gone |
| nous étions allé(e)s | we had gone |
| vous étiez allé(e)(s) | you had gone |
| ils étaient allés | they had gone |
| elles étaient allées | they had gone |

### Now try this

Look at the verbs in the highlighted expressions. What tense are they in: pluperfect, imperfect or perfect?

Pendant les vacances de neige, mes parents (1) avaient loué un appartement près des pistes de ski.

(2) J'avais toujours voulu apprendre à faire du ski.

Ma sœur (3) avait déjà fait un stage, mais moi, (4) je n'en avais jamais fait.

(5) J'avais passé des heures devant mon ordinateur pour choisir le meilleur équipement.

(6) J'avais regardé des DVD d'apprentissage de ski. (7) Je savais, en principe, comment descendre des pistes de toutes les couleurs, mais le premier jour. (8) je suis sorti et plouf … (9) je suis tombé et (10) je me suis cassé la jambe. (11) Je ne m'attendais pas à passer les vacances à l'hôpital!

# Negatives

You need to be able to understand and use negatives to aim for a higher grade in all parts of your exam.

## Negative expressions

| | |
|---|---|
| ne … pas | not |
| ne … jamais | never |
| ne … plus | no longer, not any more |
| ne … rien | nothing, not anything |
| ne … personne | nobody, not anybody |
| ne … guère | hardly |
| ne … aucun(e) | not any |
| ne … que | only |
| ne … ni … ni … | neither … nor |

## Formation

You know that negatives are made by making a ne … pas sandwich around the verb.

The ne is a marker to tell you that a negative is coming …

## Word order

- Personne can also come in front of the verb:

  Personne n'est venu.   No one came.

- When the verb has two parts, the negative forms the sandwich around the auxiliary:

  Je ne suis jamais allé(e) en France.
  I have never been to France.

- If there is a pronoun before the auxiliary it is included in the sandwich:

  Je n'y suis jamais allé(e).
  I've never been there.

- If there are two verbs, the sandwich goes around the first verb:

  Je ne veux pas y aller.
  I don't want to go there.

  Nous ne pouvons pas télécharger l'appli sans un mot de passe.   We can't download the app without a password.

- If there is a reflexive pronoun, that is included in the sandwich too:

  Ils ne s'entendent pas bien.
  They don't get on well.

## Now try this

1 Match the French negative sentences with the English ones on the right.
  1 Il ne mange pas de viande.
  2 On m'a dit que tu ne fumes plus.
  3 Manon n'a jamais  mangé d'escargots.
  4 Nous ne voulons plus rien.
  5 Je n'ai vu personne.
  6 Elle n'a aucun doute.
  7 Il n'a que dix ans.
  8 D'où vient-elle? Elle n'est ni italienne ni espagnole.

  a We don't want anything else.
  b Manon has never eaten snails.
  c I didn't see anyone.
  d He's only ten.
  e She has no doubts.
  f Someone told me you don't smoke any more.
  g Where's she from? She's neither Italian nor Spanish.
  h He doesn't eat meat.

2 Make negative sentences with the expressions provided.
  (a) Tu fais (ne … rien).
  (b) Tu m'as aidé à la maison (ne … jamais).
  (c) Tu fais tes devoirs (ne … plus).
  (d) Tu respectes (ne … personne).
  (e) Tu fais le nécessaire (ne … que).
  (f) Tu peux aller au football ou au restaurant ce soir (ne … ni … ni …).

101

# Questions

You won't get very far if you can't ask questions, so make sure you know how to!

## Ways of asking questions

You can ask a 'yes' and 'no' question in three ways:

**1** Change a statement into a question by raising your voice at the end of the sentence:
Tu vas en ville?
This is the most popular way.

**2** Put est-ce que at the start of the sentence ('is it that ...?').
Est-ce que tu vas en ville?
This is probably the easiest way.

**3** Swap around the subject and verb.
Vas-tu en ville?
Va-t-il en ville?
This is not used as much as it used to be. You should be able to recognise it but you won't be expected to use it.

Qu'est-ce que tu fais?
What are you doing?

## Question words

The other way to ask a question is to start with a question word:

| | |
|---|---|
| Qui? | Who? |
| Quand? | When? |
| Où? | Where? |
| Comment? | How? |
| Combien de? | How many? |
| À quelle heure? | At what time? |
| Pourquoi? | Why? |
| Que? | What? |
| Depuis quand? | Since when? |

Question words can be followed by est-ce que:

Où est-ce que tu habites?
Where do you live?

Comment est-ce que tu vas au collège?
How do you get to school?

À quelle heure est-ce que tu te lèves?
What time do you get up?

Pourquoi est-ce que tu ne te lèves pas plus tôt?
Why don't you get up earlier?

Depuis quand est-ce que tu habites ici?
How long have you lived here?

Qu'est-ce que tu aimes faire?
What do you like doing?

## Now try this

Match up the two part of each question so that they make sense. Then translate the questions into English.

| | |
|---|---|
| Où | apprends-tu le français? |
| Qui | rentrent tes parents? |
| Comment | voulez-vous faire? |
| Combien | allez-vous? |
| À quelle heure | travaille ton père? |
| Pourquoi | as-tu raté le bus? |
| Que | d'amis as-tu sur Facebook? |
| Depuis quand | va à la fête? |

# Useful little words

Prepositions and conjunctions are very useful little words for making your speaking and writing clear and accurate.

## Prepositions

Some prepositions tell you WHERE something is:

| | |
|---|---|
| à côté de | beside |
| dans | in |
| derrière | behind |
| devant | in front of |
| dehors | outside |
| en face de | opposite |
| entre | between |
| loin de | far from |
| près de | near to |
| partout | everywhere |
| sous | under |
| sur | on |
| vers | towards |

Note that the de changes to du, de la, de l' or des, depending on the noun that follows.

| | |
|---|---|
| à côté du cinéma | next to the cinema |
| en face de la gare | opposite the station |
| près de l'école | near to the school |
| près des magasins | near to the shops |

Others are just useful little words:

| | |
|---|---|
| à | at / to |
| avec | with |
| chez | at the house of ... |
| en | in / at |
| environ | about |
| jusqu'à | up to / until |
| sans | without |
| sauf | except |

### Verbs with prepositions

Some common verbs take a preposition before another infinitive:

| | |
|---|---|
| décider de sortir | to decide to go out |
| apprendre à conduire | to learn to drive |
| réussir à faire ... | to succeed in doing ... |
| oublier de faire ... | to forget to do ... |

## Saying 'in' or 'to' with places

To say 'in' or 'to' a town or country:

• Use en before the names of feminine countries (most countries are feminine):
Elle va en France.   She's going to France.

• Use au before masculine countries:
J'habite au pays de Galles.   I live in Wales.

• Use à before the name of a town:
J'habite à Paris.   I live in Paris.

## Useful conjunctions

Use conjunctions to combine short sentences.

| | | | | | | | |
|---|---|---|---|---|---|---|---|
| d'abord | at first | aussi | also / as well | puis | then | et | and |
| au début | at the start | donc | so / then | ensuite | next | mais | but |
| alors | then | à la fin | at the end | ou | or | | |

## Now try this

Choose a suitable preposition or conjunction from the box to fill each gap.

Je me sentais triste. Mon chat avait disparu! J'avais cherché (1) .................. J'avais cherché (2) .................. le lit, (3) .................. le placard, (4) .................. la porte. (5) .................. j'ai eu une idée, je suis allé (6) .................. et j'ai cherché (7) .................. le jardin, mais (8) .................. succès. (9) .................. je suis rentré (10) .................. ma chambre. Je suis allé (11) .................. lit. Je l'ai vu! Il était (12) .................. les draps.

sous  puis  dans  au  sans  à  partout  à la fin  dehors  ensuite  sous  dans  derrière

# Useful bits and pieces

## Numbers

| | | |
|---|---|---|
| 1 un | 11 onze | 21 vingt-et-un |
| 2 deux | 12 douze | 22 vingt-deux |
| 3 trois | 13 treize | 23 vingt-trois |
| 4 quatre | 14 quatorze | 24 vingt-quatre |
| 5 cinq | 15 quinze | 25 vingt-cinq |
| 6 six | 16 seize | 26 vingt-six |
| 7 sept | 17 dix-sept | 27 vingt-sept |
| 8 huit | 18 dix-huit | 28 vingt-huit |
| 9 neuf | 19 dix-neuf | 29 vingt-neuf |
| 10 dix | 20 vingt | 30 trente |

| | |
|---|---|
| 40 quarante | 100 cent |
| 50 cinquante | 200 deux-cents |
| 60 soixante | 1000 mille |
| 70 soixante-dix | 2000 deux-mille |
| 80 quatre-vingts | |
| 90 quatre-vingt-dix | |

## Dates and festivals

**Days of the week**

lundi mardi mercredi jeudi vendredi samedi dimanche

**Months of the year**

janvier février mars avril mai juin juillet août septembre octobre novembre décembre

**The seasons**

le printemps    l'été    l'automne    l'hiver

| | |
|---|---|
| le premier juin | 1st June |
| le deux avril | 2nd April |
| le trente-et-un mars | 31st March |
| les jours fériés | holidays |
| Noël | Christmas |
| le Nouvel An | New Year |
| la Saint-Sylvestre | New Year's Eve |
| Pâques | Easter |

## Intensifiers

| | |
|---|---|
| très | very |
| Il est très grand. | He is very big. |
| peu | a bit |
| Elle est un peu timide. | She's a bit shy. |
| trop | too |
| Nous sommes trop fatigués. | We are too tired. |
| assez | quite |
| J'ai assez mangé. | I'm full. (I've eaten enough.) |
| beaucoup | much / many |
| Merci beaucoup. | Many thanks. |

## Time

Quelle heure est-il?    What time is it?

Il est huit heures et demie.

Il est neuf heures et quart.

Il est dix heures moins le quart.

Il est midi / minuit.

## Quantities

| | |
|---|---|
| assez de | enough (of) |
| beaucoup de | much / many (of) |
| plusieur | several |
| un morceau de | a piece of |
| un paquet de | a packet of |
| un pot de | a jar / tub of |
| un tiers de | a third of |
| une moitié de | a half of |

| | |
|---|---|
| une boîte de | a box / tin of |
| une bouteille de | a bottle of |
| une cannette | a (drinks) can |
| une douzaine de | a dozen (of) |
| une tranche de | a slice (of) |
| un kilo de | a kilo of |
| une livre de | half a kilo of |
| un régime de bananes | a bunch of bananas |

# Vocabulary

This section starts with general terms that are useful in a wide variety of situations and then divides into vocabulary for each of the four main topics covered in this revision guide:

**1** High frequency vocabulary    **3** Out and about      **5** Future plans, education and work

**2** Personal information    **4** Customer service and transactions

Learning vocabulary is essential preparation for your reading and listening exams. Don't try to learn too much at once – concentrate on learning and testing yourself on a page at a time.

## **1** High frequency language

### Question words

| | |
|---|---|
| à quelle heure? | (at) what time? |
| comment? | how? |
| combien de ...? | how much ...?, how many ...? |
| de quelle couleur? | what colour? |
| où? | where? |
| pourquoi? | why? |
| quel / quelle ...? | what / which ...? (singular item, m/f) |
| quels / quelles ...? | what / which ...? (plural item, m/f) |
| que ...? | what ...? |
| quoi? | what? |
| qu'est-ce qui ...? | what? (as subject) |
| qu'est-ce que ...? | what? (as object) |
| quand? | when? |
| qui? | who? |

### Quantities

| | |
|---|---|
| assez de | enough |
| beaucoup de | a lot of, many |
| demi | half |
| encore de | more |
| moins de | less |
| moitié (f) | half |
| pas mal de | quite a few |
| plein de | a lot of |
| plus de | more |
| plusieurs | several |
| quelques | some |
| trop de | too many |
| un kilo de | a kilo of |
| un litre de | a litre of |
| un morceau de | a piece of |
| un paquet de | a packet of |
| un peu de | a little of / few |
| un pot de | a jar of |
| un tiers de | a third of |
| une boîte de | a tin / box of |
| une bouteille de | a bottle of |
| une douzaine de | a dozen |
| une tranche de | a slice of |

### Connecting words

| | |
|---|---|
| d'abord | first |
| alors | then |
| aussi | also |
| car | because |
| donc | so |
| enfin | finally, at last |
| ensuite | then |
| et | and |
| finalement | finally |
| mais | but |
| même si | even if |
| ou | or |
| parce que | because |
| puis | then |
| puisque | since |
| si | if |
| tout d'abord | first of all |

### Days of the week

| | |
|---|---|
| lundi | jeudi |
| mardi | vendredi |
| mercredi | samedi |
| | dimanche |

### Months of the year

| | |
|---|---|
| janvier | January |
| février | February |
| mars | March |
| avril | April |
| mai | May |
| juin | June |
| juillet | July |
| août | August |
| septembre | September |
| octobre | October |
| novembre | November |
| décembre | December |

### Other expressions

| | |
|---|---|
| à moi | mine |
| à mon avis | in my opinion |
| avec plaisir | with pleasure |
| bien sûr | of course |
| bof | don't care! |
| bonne chance | good luck |
| ça dépend | it depends |
| ça m'énerve | it annoys me |
| ça m'est égal | I don't mind |
| ça me fait rire | it makes me laugh |
| ça me plaît | I like it |
| ça ne fait rien | it doesn't matter |
| ça ne me dit rien | that doesn't interest me |
| ça s'écrit comment? | how do you spell that? |
| ça suffit | that's enough |
| ça va | I'm fine |
| d'accord | okay |
| d'habitude | usually |
| défense de | you are not allowed to |
| encore une fois | once again |
| être en train de | to be in the middle of |
| être sur le point de | to be about to |
| il est interdit de | it is forbidden to, you are not allowed to |
| il faut | it is necessary to, you must |
| il y a | there is, there are |
| j'en ai assez / marre | I've had enough |
| personnellement | personally |
| quel dommage | what a shame |
| tant mieux | all the better |
| tant pis | too bad |
| voici | here you are |
| voilà | there you are |

### Now try this

Practise days and months by translating the birthdays of family and friends into French.

# ❶ High frequency language

## Prepositions

| | |
|---|---|
| à | at, to |
| à cause de | because of |
| à côté de | next to |
| après | after |
| au bout de | at the end of |
| autour de | around |
| avant | before |
| avec | with |
| chez | at (someone's house) |
| contre | against |
| dans | in |
| de | from |
| dehors | outside |
| derrière | behind |
| devant | in front of |
| en | in, by |
| en face de | opposite |
| en haut | above |
| entre | between |
| environ | about |
| jusqu'à | until |
| loin de | far from |
| nulle part | nowhere |
| par | through |
| parmi | among |
| partout | everywhere |
| pendant | during |
| pour | for, in order |
| près de | near |
| quelque part | somewhere |
| sans | without |
| sauf | except |
| selon | according to |
| sous | under |
| sur | on |
| vers | towards |

## Time expressions

| | |
|---|---|
| à l'heure | on time |
| à partir de | from |
| après | after |
| après-demain | the day after tomorrow |
| après-midi (m) | afternoon |
| au début | at the start |
| aujourd'hui | today |
| avant | before |
| avant-hier | the day before yesterday |
| bientôt | soon |
| de bonne heure | on time, early |
| de temps en temps | from time to time |
| déjà | already |
| demain | tomorrow |
| depuis | since |
| deux fois | twice |
| en même temps | at the same time |
| hier | yesterday |
| hier soir | last night |
| jour (m) | day |
| journée (f) | day |
| lendemain (m) | the next day |
| maintenant | now |
| matin (m) | morning |
| minuit | midnight |
| minute (f) | minute |
| nuit (f) | night |
| pendant | during, for |
| plus tard | later |
| prochain(e) | next |
| quinzaine (f) | a fortnight |
| quinze jours | a fortnight |
| semaine (f) | week |
| soir (m) | evening |
| soirée (f) | evening, party |
| toujours | always |
| tous les jours | every day |
| tout à l'heure | just now, in a little while |
| une fois | once |
| veille (f) | the night before |
| weekend (m) | weekend |

## Verbs A–D

| | |
|---|---|
| accepter | to accept |
| accompagner | to accompany |
| acheter | to buy |
| adorer | to love |
| aider | to help |
| aimer | to like |
| ajouter | to add |
| allumer | to switch on, light |
| améliorer | to improve |
| annuler | to cancel |
| appeler | to call |
| apprendre | to learn |
| arriver | to arrive |
| attendre | to wait for |
| atterrir | to land |
| avoir | to have |
| bavarder | to chat |
| boire | to drink |
| changer | to change |
| charger | to load, charge |
| choisir | to choose |
| cliquer | to click |
| coller | to stick |
| commander | to order |
| commencer | to begin |
| comprendre | to understand |
| compter | to count, intend |
| conduire | to drive |
| connaître | to know (be familiar with) |
| conseiller | to advise |
| contacter | to contact |
| coûter | to cost |
| croire | to think, believe |
| décider | to decide |
| décrire | to describe |
| demander | to ask |
| dépenser | to spend |
| descendre | to go down |
| désirer | to want, desire |
| détester | to hate |
| devoir | to have to |
| dire | to say |
| discuter | to discuss |
| donner | to give |
| dormir | to sleep |
| durer | to last |

## Now try this

Test yourself on the time expressions above by covering up the English column and then writing down the English translations yourself. Compare your answers with the list above. How many have you got right?

# ❶ High frequency language

## Verbs E–P

| écouter | to listen |
|---|---|
| écrire | to write |
| empêcher | to prevent |
| emprunter | to borrow |
| entendre | to hear |
| entrer | to enter / to go in |
| envoyer | to send |
| espérer | to hope |
| essayer | to try |
| être | to be |
| étudier | to study |
| fermer | to close, switch off |
| finir | to finish, end |
| frapper | to knock, hit |
| gagner | to win, earn |
| garer | to park |
| habiter | to live |
| informer | to inform |
| introduire | to introduce |
| inviter | to invite |
| jeter | to throw |
| laisser | to leave (an object) |
| louer | to rent, hire |
| manger | to eat |
| manquer | to miss |
| marcher | to walk |
| mériter | to deserve |
| mettre | to put |
| monter | to climb, go up, get on |
| montrer | to show |
| neiger | to snow |
| noter | to note |
| offrir | to give (presents) |
| organiser | to organise |
| oublier | to forget |
| ouvrir | to open |
| pardonner | to forgive |
| parler | to speak |
| partir | to leave |
| passer | to take (an exam) |
| penser | to think |
| perdre | to lose |
| permettre | to allow |

## Verbs P–S

| plaire | to please |
|---|---|
| pleurer | to cry |
| poser une question | to ask a question |
| pousser | to push |
| pouvoir | to be able to |
| préférer | to prefer |
| prendre | to take |
| présenter | to present |
| prêter | to lend |
| prévenir | to warn |
| produire | to produce |
| quitter | to leave |
| raconter | to tell |
| rater | to go wrong, fail |
| recevoir | to receive, be host to |
| rechercher | to research |
| recommander | to recommend |
| regretter | to regret, be sorry |
| rembourser | to refund |
| remercier | to thank |
| remettre | to put back |
| remplacer | to replace |
| remplir | to fill |
| rencontrer | to meet |
| rendre visite à | to visit (a person) |
| rentrer | to return |
| réparer | to repair |
| répéter | to repeat |
| répondre | to answer, reply |
| réserver | to reserve |
| ressembler à | to look like, resemble |
| rester | to stay |
| retourner | to return |
| réussir | to succeed, to pass an exam |
| réviser | to revise |
| rire | to laugh |
| rouler | to go along (in a car) |
| s'adresser à | to apply to |
| s'amuser | to enjoy oneself |
| s'appeler | to be called |
| s'arrêter | to stop |

## Verbs S–Z

| s'asseoir | to sit down |
|---|---|
| s'échapper | to escape |
| s'ennuyer | to be bored |
| s'intéresser à | to be interested in |
| s'occuper de | to look after |
| sauter | to jump |
| sauver | to save |
| savoir | to know (a fact) |
| se débrouiller | to manage, deal with things |
| se dépêcher | to hurry |
| se disputer | to argue |
| se fâcher | to get angry |
| se promener | to go for a walk |
| se rappeler | to remember |
| se servir de | to use |
| se souvenir | to remember |
| se taire | to be quiet |
| se terminer | to end |
| se trouver | to be located |
| sembler | to seem |
| servir | to serve |
| signer | to sign |
| sonner | to ring |
| souhaiter | to wish |
| sourire | to smile |
| stationner | to park |
| suivre | to follow |
| surfer sur internet | to surf the internet |
| taper | to type |
| téléphoner | to phone |
| tenir | to hold |
| tirer | to pull |
| tomber | to fall |
| toucher | to touch |
| travailler | to work |
| trouver | to find |
| utiliser | to use |
| vendre | to sell |
| venir | to come |
| vérifier | to check |
| visiter | to visit (a place) |
| vivre | to live |
| voir | to see |
| voler | to steal, fly |
| vouloir | to want |

**Now try this**

Pick five verbs from each column and put them into the present, perfect and future tenses for the **je** form. Check your answers by looking at pages 89–98.

# ❶ High frequency language

## Adjectives A–G

| | |
|---|---|
| affreux/euse | awful |
| ancien(ne) | old, former |
| autre | other |
| beau / bel / belle | beautiful |
| bon(ne) | good |
| bref / brève | brief |
| bruyant | noisy |
| cadet(te) | younger |
| cassé(e) | broken |
| chaud(e) | hot |
| cher / chère | expensive / dear |
| chouette | great |
| comique | comical |
| compliqué(e) | complicated |
| confiant(e) | confident |
| confortable | comfortable |
| content(e) | happy, pleased |
| correct(e) | correct |
| court(e) | short |
| dégoûtant | disgusting |
| dernier/ière | last |
| désolé(e) | sorry |
| difficile | difficult |
| dur | hard |
| dynamique | dynamic |
| éducatif/ive | educational |
| embêtant | annoying |
| en colère | angry |
| énervant | annoying |
| ennuyeux/euse | boring |
| énorme | enormous |
| ensemble | together |
| étonné(e) | surprised |
| fâché | angry |
| facile | easy |
| faible | weak |
| fatigant | tiring |
| fatigué(e) | tired |
| faux / fausse | false |
| favori(te) | favourite |
| fermé(e) | closed |
| formidable | great, marvellous |
| fort(e) | strong |
| génial(e) | great, brilliant |
| grand(e) | big, tall |
| gratuit(e) | free |
| gros(se) | fat |

## Adjectives H–R

| | |
|---|---|
| haut(e) | high |
| heureux/euse | happy |
| incroyable | unbelievable |
| injuste | unfair |
| inquiet / inquiète | worried |
| insatisfait(e) | dissatisfied |
| inutile | useless |
| jeune | young |
| joli(e) (e) | pretty |
| juste | fair |
| laid | ugly |
| léger / légère | light |
| libre | free |
| long(ue) | long |
| lourd(e) | heavy |
| magnifique | magnificent |
| malheureux/euse | unhappy |
| mauvais(e) | bad |
| merveilleux/euse | marvellous |
| moche | ugly, rotten |
| mûr | mature |
| nécessaire | necessary |
| neuf / neuve | new (brand new) |
| nombreux/euse | numerous |
| nouveau / nouvel / nouvelle | new |
| nul(le) | rubbish |
| ouvert(e) | open |
| parfait(e) | perfect |
| pas cher / chère | cheap |
| perdu(e) | lost |
| pessimiste | pessimistic |
| petit(e) | small |
| préféré(e) | favourite |
| premier/ière | first |
| pressé(e) | in a hurry |
| prêt | ready |
| prochain(e) | next |
| proche | close |
| propre | clean, own |
| récent(e) | recent |
| recherché(e) | sought after |
| reconnaissant(e) | grateful |
| reconnu(e) | recognised / well known |
| réel(le) | real |
| responsable | responsible |
| rigolo(te) | funny |

## Adjectives S–Z

| | |
|---|---|
| sale | dirty |
| satisfait(e) | satisfied |
| sensass | sensational |
| seul(e) | alone |
| sévère | strict |
| silencieux/ieuse | silent |
| simple | easy |
| super | great |
| sûr (de moi etc) | confident |
| surpris(e) | surprised |
| tranquille | calm, quiet |
| travailleur/euse | hardworking |
| triste | sad |
| typique | typical |
| utile | useful |
| valable | valid |
| vieux / vieil / vieille | old |
| vrai(e) | true |

## Adverbs

| | |
|---|---|
| d'habitude | usually |
| déjà | already |
| encore | more |
| ici | here |
| immédiatement | immediately |
| là | there |
| là-bas | over there |
| là-haut | up there |
| longtemps | (for a) long time |
| malheureusement | unfortunately |
| normalement | usually |
| peut-être | perhaps |
| plutôt | rather |
| pourtant | however |
| presque | almost |
| quelquefois | sometimes |
| rarement | rarely |
| récemment | recently |
| souvent | often |
| surtout | especially |
| toujours | always, still |
| tout de suite | straight away |
| très | very |
| trop | too |
| vite | quickly |
| vraiment | really |

## Now try this

Choose ten key adjectives and make learning cards for them. Write the French word on one side and a picture or the English meaning on the other. Then test yourself on your chosen adjectives.

# ❷ Personal information

## Family members

| | |
|---|---|
| beau-fils (m) | stepson / son-in-law |
| belle-fille (f) | stepdaughter / daughter-in-law |
| beau-père (m) | stepfather / father-in-law |
| belle-mère (f) | stepmother / mother-in-law |
| bébé (m) | baby |
| demi-frère (m) | half-brother |
| demi-sœur (f) | half-sister |
| enfant (m/f) | child |
| enfant unique (m/f) | only child |
| famille (f) | family |
| fille (f) | daughter / girl |
| fils (m) | son |
| frère (m) | brother |
| frères et sœurs (m/pl) | brothers and sisters / siblings |
| garçon (m) | boy |
| grand-mère (f) | grandmother |
| grand-père (m) | grandfather |
| grands-parents (m/pl) | grandparents |
| jumeaux (m/pl) | twins |
| jumelles (f/pl) | twins |
| maman (f) | mum |
| mamie / mémé (f) | granny |
| mère (f) | mother |
| homme (m) | man |
| mari (m) | husband |
| oncle (m) | uncle |
| papa (m) | dad |
| papy / pépé (m) | granddad |
| parents (m/pl) | parents |
| père (m) | father |
| sœur | sister |
| tante | aunt |
| voisin(e) (m/f) | neighbour |

**H** (HIGHER)

| | |
|---|---|
| personne âgée (f) | pensioner |
| petit-fils (m) | grandson |
| petite-fille (f) | granddaughter |
| vrais jumeaux | identical twins |

## Character description

| | |
|---|---|
| agaçant(e) | annoying |
| agréable | pleasant |
| aimable | likeable |
| aîné(e) | older, oldest (brother / sister) |
| amical(e) | friendly |
| amusant(e) | funny, humorous |
| autoritaire | bossy |
| aventureux/euse | adventurous |
| beau / belle | beautiful, handsome |
| bête | silly, foolish |
| bavard(e) | chatty, talkative |
| calme | quiet |
| charmant(e) | charming |
| de bonne / mauvaise humeur | in a good / bad mood |
| démodé(e) | old-fashioned |
| désagréable | unpleasant |
| drôle | funny, witty |
| effronté(e) | cheeky |
| égoïste | selfish |
| énergique | energetic |
| énervant(e) | annoying |
| gentil(le) | nice, kind |
| honnête | honest |
| impatient(e) | impatient |
| impoli(e) | impolite |
| insupportable | unbearable |
| intelligent(e) | intelligent |
| méchant(e) | mean, nasty |
| marrant(e) | funny |
| mignon(ne) | pretty |
| mince | thin |
| optimiste | optimistic |
| paresseux/euse | lazy |
| patient(e) | patient |
| pessimiste | pessimistic |
| raisonnable | reasonable, sensible |
| sage | well-behaved |
| sensible | sensitive |
| sérieux/euse | serious |
| sympa | nice, likeable, friendly |
| têtu(e) | stubborn |
| timide | shy |

**H** (HIGHER)

| | |
|---|---|
| confiant(e) | self-confident |
| énerver | to annoy |
| généreux/euse | generous |
| indépendant(e) | independent |
| le sens de l'humour | a sense of humour |

## Pets

| | |
|---|---|
| animal domestique (m) | pet |

chat (m)

chien (m)

cochon d'Inde (m)

lapin (m)

poisson rouge (m)

poisson tropical (m)

## Now try this

To help you learn the personality adjectives, write out the French words in three lists: positive, negative and neutral. Then memorise five adjectives that could describe you.

# ② Personal information

## Leisure activities

| alpinisme (m) | mountaineering |
| arts martiaux (m/pl) | martial arts |
| athlétisme (m) | athletics |
| basket (m) | basketball |
| boxe (f) | boxing |
| canoë-kayak (m) | canoeing |
| cyclisme (m) | cycling |
| équitation (f) | horse-riding |
| faire de la natation | to swim |
| faire de la voile | to sail |
| faire des randonnées | to go hiking / walking |
| faire du cheval | to go horse-riding |
| faire du patin à glace | to ice-skate |
| faire du patin à roulettes | to roller-skate |
| faire une promenade | to go for a walk |
| faire du roller / skateboard | to rollerblade / skateboard |
| faire du sport | to do sport |
| gymnastique (f) | gymnastics |
| nager | to swim |
| natation (f) | swimming |
| pêcher | to fish |
| ski (nautique) (m) | (water) skiing |
| tennis (m) | tennis |
| tennis de table (m) | table tennis |
| trampoline (m) | trampolining |
| sports d'hiver (m/pl) | winter sports |
| surf (m) | surfing |

 HIGHER H

| aviron (m) | rowing |
| escalade (f) | rock climbing |
| escrime (f) | fencing |
| parapente (f) | paragliding |
| parachutage (m) | parachuting |
| planche à voile (f) | windsurfing |
| plongée sous-marine (f) | scuba diving |
| sports extrêmes (m/pl) | extreme sports |
| tir à l'arc (m) | archery |

il fait du kayak

il joue au football

je fais du trampoline

je fais du vélo

elle fait du cheval

## Musical instruments

| batterie (f) | drums |
| clarinette (f) | clarinet |
| clavier (électronique) (m) | keyboard |
| flûte (f) | flute |
| flûte à bec (f) | recorder |
| guitare (f) | guitar |
| orchestre (m) | orchestra |
| piano (m) | piano |
| saxophone / saxo (m) | saxophone |
| trompette (f) | trumpet |
| violon (m) | violin |

## General terms

| accompagner | to go along, to accompany |
| activité (f) | activity |
| aérobic (m) | aerobics |
| baskets (f/pl) | trainers |
| billet d'entrée (m) | ticket |
| but (m) | goal |
| centre sportif (m) | sports centre |
| championnat (m) | championship |
| classique | classical, classic |
| club des jeunes (m) | youth club |
| console de jeux (f) | games console |
| danse (f) | dancing |
| danser | to dance |
| échecs (m/pl) | chess |
| équipe (f) | team |

| équipement sportif (m) | sports equipment |
| jeu vidéo (m) | computer game |
| maillot (de sport) (m) | sports shirt |
| maison des jeunes (f) | youth club |
| musique (f) | music |
| passe-temps (m) | leisure activity |
| pièce (de théâtre) (f) | play (at the theatre) |
| scène (f) | stage |
| s'entraîner | to train |
| se relaxer | to relax |
| se reposer | to rest |
| se promener | to go for a walk |
| séance (f) | performance |
| short (m) | shorts |
| sortir | to go out |
| surf (m) | surfing |
| survêtement (m) | tracksuit |
| tenue de sport (f) | sports kit |
| terrain de sport (m) | sports ground |

 HIGHER H

| bavarder | to chat |
| faire du lèche-vitrines | to go window shopping |
| passionnant | exciting |
| tournoi (m) | tournament |

**Now try this**

Draw stickmen doing the sports listed and label them, to help memorise the words and how to spell them.

# ❷ Personal information

## Lifestyle

| | |
|---|---|
| bio(logique) | organic |
| boire | to drink |
| boisson (f) | drink |
| bonbons (m/pl) | sweets |
| eau (minérale) (f) | (mineral) water |
| en bonne santé | healthy |
| en forme | fit |
| faire de l'aérobic | to do aerobics |
| faire de l'exercice | to exercise, work out |
| faire du jogging | to jog |
| faire du sport | to do sport |
| faire une promenade | to go for a walk |
| garder la forme | to keep fit |
| gros(se) | fat |
| grossir | to put on weight |
| maigrir | to lose weight |
| malsain | unhealthy |
| nourriture (f) | food |
| pas en forme | unfit |
| perdre du poids | to lose weight |
| plein de goût | tasty |
| plus âgé(e) | older |
| prendre du poids | to put on weight |
| prendre le petit déjeuner | to have / eat breakfast |
| santé (f) | health |
| suivre un régime | to be on a diet |
| vitamines (f/pl) | vitamins |
| yaourt (m) | yoghurt |

| | |
|---|---|
| allégé(e) | low fat |
| boissons sucrées (f/pl) | fizzy drinks |
| équilibré(e) | balanced |
| être en forme | to be fit |
| nourriture bio (f) | organic food |
| résister à la tentation | to resist temptation |
| s'habituer à | to get used to |

## Ailments

| | |
|---|---|
| aller mieux | to feel better |
| avoir chaud | to be hot |
| avoir de la fièvre | to have a temperature |
| avoir faim | to be hungry |
| avoir froid | to be cold |
| avoir mal à | to have -ache |
| avoir peur | to be afraid |
| avoir soif | to be thirsty |
| blesser | to injure |
| blessure (f) | injury |
| ça me fait mal | that hurts |
| cabinet de médecin (m) | doctor's surgery |
| dent (f) | tooth |
| dentiste (m/f) | dentist |
| comprimé (m) | tablet |
| estomac (m) | stomach |
| faire mal | to hurt |
| faire mal à | to harm / injure |
| garder le lit | to stay in bed |
| grave | serious (illness) |
| grippe (f) | flu |
| infirmier / ière (m/f) | nurse |
| malade | ill, sick |
| médecin (m) | doctor |
| médicament (m) | medicine |
| prendre rendez-vous | to make an appointment |
| prendre un médicament | to take medicine |
| remède (f) | remedy, medicine |
| rendez-vous (m) | appointment |
| température (f) | temperature |
| tousser | to cough |

| | |
|---|---|
| avoir la tête qui tourne | to be dizzy |
| date limite de consommation (f) | use-by date |
| vomir | to be sick, vomit |

## Health issues

| | |
|---|---|
| abandonner | to give up |
| alcool (m) | alcohol |
| alcoolique | alcoholic |
| arrêter | to stop |
| arrêter de fumer | to stop smoking |
| avertir | to warn |
| cigarette (f) | cigarette |
| drogue (f) | drug |
| fumer | to smoke |
| fumeur / euse (m/f) | smoker |
| non-alcoolisé(e) | non-alcoholic |

| | |
|---|---|
| accroché(e) | addicted |
| alcoolique (m/f) | alcoholic (person) |
| alcoolisme (m) | alcoholism |
| anoréxique | anorexic |
| cancer (m) | cancer |
| centre de désintoxication (m) | rehab centre |
| centre des addictions (m) | drug advice centre |
| crise cardiaque (f) | heart attack |
| dépendance (f) | addiction |
| dépendant(e) | dependent |
| drogues (f/pl) | drugs |
| drogué(e) (m/f) | drug addict |
| séropositif / ive | HIV-positive |
| sida (m) | AIDS |

## Parts of the body

| | |
|---|---|
| bras (m) | arm |
| corps (m) | body |
| dents (f/pl) | teeth |
| doigt (m) | finger |
| dos (m) | back |
| épaule (f) | shoulder |
| estomac (m) | stomach |
| genou (m) | knee |
| gorge (f) | throat |
| jambe (f) | leg |
| main (f) | hand |
| pied (m) | foot |
| tête (f) | head |
| yeux (m/pl) | eyes |

## Now try this

Draw a body and see if you can label it in French.

111

# ❸ Out and about

## Visitor information

|  |  |
|---|---|
| à l'étranger | abroad |
| à l'extérieur | outside |
| à l'intérieur | inside |
| accueil (m) | welcome |
| affiche (f) | poster / notice |
| attraction touristique (f) | tourist attraction |
| au bord de la mer | at the seaside |
| bon séjour | enjoy your stay |
| bon voyage | have a good journey |
| bureau d'accueil / de renseignements (m) | tourist information office |
| bureau des objets trouvés (m) | lost property office |
| carte d'identité (f) | identity card |
| carte postale (f) | postcard |
| carte routière (f) | road map |
| centre-ville (m) | town centre |
| composter | to validate a ticket |
| exposition (f) | exhibition |
| fermeture (f) | closing |
| fête (f) | feast / fair / festival |
| fiche (f) | form |
| frontière (f) | border |
| jour de fête (m) | public holiday |
| jour férié (m) | bank holiday |
| liste des hôtels (f) | hotel list |
| location (f) | hiring / renting |
| logement (m) | accommodation |
| loin | far |
| louer | to rent |
| montagne (f) | mountain |
| ouvert | open |
| plan de la ville (m) | town map |
| recommander | to recommend |
| région (f) | area / region |
| spectacle (m) | show |
| visite guidée (f) | guided tour |

le nord
l'ouest —— l'est
le sud

**HIGHER H**

|  |  |
|---|---|
| avoir lieu | to take place |
| heures de pointe (f/pl) | rush hour |
| vacances de neige (f/pl) | winter / skiing holiday |
| voyage organisé (m) | package holiday |

## Weather

|  |  |
|---|---|
| saison (f) | season |
| au printemps | in spring |
| en automne | in autumn |
| en été | in summer |
| en hiver | in winter |
| dans l'est / à l'est de | in the east |
| dans l'ouest / à l'ouest de | in the west |
| dans le nord / au nord de | in the north |
| dans le sud / au sud de | in the south |
| il fait beau | it's fine / nice weather |
| il fait chaud | it's hot |
| il fait froid | it's cold |
| il fait / il y a du soleil | the sun is shining |
| il gèle | it's freezing |
| il fait mauvais | it's bad weather |
| il neige | it's snowing |
| il pleut | it's raining |
| il y a des éclairs | there's lightning |
| il y a / il fait du tonnerre | it's thundering |
| briller | to shine |
| brouillard (m) | fog |

|  |  |
|---|---|
| chaleur (f) | heat |
| changer | to change |
| ciel (m) | sky |
| clair | bright |
| climat (m) | climate |
| couvert | cloudy, overcast |
| degrés (m/pl) | degrees |
| éclaircie (f) | bright spell |
| ensoleillé | sunny |
| grêle (f) | hail |
| incertain | changeable |
| météo (f) | weather report |
| mouillé | wet |
| neige (f) | snow |
| nuage (m) | cloud |
| nuageux | cloudy |
| orage (m) | storm |
| pleuvoir | to rain |
| pluie (f) | rain |
| sec | dry |
| soleil (m) | sun |
| température maximale / minimale (f) | highest / lowest temperature |
| temps (m) | weather |
| vent (m) | wind |
| variable | changeable |

**HIGHER H**

|  |  |
|---|---|
| averses (f/pl) | showers |
| prévisions météo (f/pl) | weather forecast |
| température moyenne (f) | average temperature |

## Now try this

Choose a holiday or trip you have been on and memorise ten words connected with that holiday or trip.

# ❸ Out and about

le stade   la cathédrale   l'avion   le train   la poste

## Local amenities

| | |
|---|---|
| aire de jeux (f) | playground |
| banque (f) | bank |
| bar (m) | pub |
| bâtiment (m) | building |
| bibliothèque (f) | library |
| boîte de nuit (f) | nightclub |
| bowling (m) | bowling alley |
| cathédrale (f) | cathedral |
| centre commercial / sportif (m) | shopping / sports centre |
| centre de loisirs (m) | leisure centre |
| château (m) | castle |
| commerce (m) | shop, business |
| commissariat (m) | police station |
| galerie d'art (f) | art gallery |
| gare routière (f) | bus station |
| gendarmerie (f) | police station |
| grand magasin (m) | department store |
| hôpital (m) | hospital |
| hôtel de ville (m) | town hall |
| immeuble (m) | tower block |
| jardin public (m) | park |
| kiosque à journaux (m) | newspaper stall |
| magasin(m) | shop |
| mairie (f) | town hall |
| marché (m) | market |
| mosquée (f) | mosque |
| musée (m) | museum |
| office de tourisme (m) | tourist office |
| patinoire (f) | ice rink |
| piscine (f) couverte / en plein air | indoor / outdoor swimming pool |
| place (f) | square |
| port (m) | port |
| station-service (f) | petrol station |
| théâtre (m) | theatre |
| usine (f) | factory |
| zone piétonne (f) | pedestrian area |

**HIGHER H**

| | |
|---|---|
| distributeur d'argent (m) | cashpoint |

## Accommodation

| | |
|---|---|
| ascenseur (m) | lift |
| bagages (m/pl) | luggage |
| baignoire (f) | bath, bathtub |
| balcon (m) | balcony |
| chambre à deux lits (f) | twin room |
| chambre double / pour deux personnes | double room |
| chambre simple / pour une personne (f) | single room |
| chauffage (m) | heating |
| clé / clef (f) | key |
| complet | full |
| compris | included |
| demi-pension (f) | half-board |
| dentrifice (m) | toothpaste |
| douche (f) | shower |
| drap (m) | sheet |
| escalier (m) | staircase |
| étage (m) | floor (1st, 2nd) |
| fonctionner | to function, work |
| gîte (m) | rented holiday house |
| gratuit | free (no cost) |
| hôte (m/f) | guest |
| inclus | included |
| lavabo (m) | washbasin |
| libre | free, available |
| linge de lit (m) | bed linen |
| logement (m) | accommodation |
| louer | to hire, to rent |
| marcher | to function, to work |
| oreiller (m) | pillow |
| pension complète (f) | full board |
| premier / deuxième étage (m) | 1st / 2nd floor |
| réception (f) | reception |
| réservation (f) | reservation |
| réserver | to book, to reserve |
| rez-de-chaussée (m) | ground floor |
| séjour (m) | overnight stay |
| serviette de bain (f) | bath towel |
| sous-sol (m) | basement |
| valise (f) | suitcase |

**HIGHER H**

| | |
|---|---|
| héberger | to put someone up |
| logé et nourri | board and lodging |
| sortie de secours (f) | emergency exit |

## Accommodation: youth hostel

| | |
|---|---|
| auberge de jeunesse (f) | youth hostel |
| cuisine (f) | kitchen |
| lit superposé (m) | bunk bed |
| parking (m) | car park |
| salle à manger (f) | dining room |
| salle de bains (f) | bathroom |
| salle de jeux (f) | games room |
| salle de séjour (f) | sitting room, lounge |
| salon (m) | sitting room, lounge |

## Accommodation: campsite

| | |
|---|---|
| à la campagne | in the country |
| accueil (m) | reception |
| aire de jeux (f) | play area |
| arrivée (f) | arrival |
| bloc sanitaire (m) | shower block |
| camper | to camp (in a tent) |
| camping (m) | campsite |
| caravane (f) | caravan |
| eau potable (f) | drinking water |
| emplacement (m) | pitch / place on campsite |
| faire du camping | to camp (in a tent) |
| ferme (f) | farm |
| sac de couchage (m) | sleeping bag |
| tente (f) | tent |

**Now try this**

Make a list in French of the amenities in your local town. You could draw a map of the town to help you remember the places.

# ❸ Out and about

## Types of transport

| | |
|---|---|
| auto (f) | car |
| avion (m) | plane |
| bateau (m) | boat |
| bateau à vapeur (m) | steamer |
| bicyclette (f) | bicycle |
| bus / autobus (m) | bus |
| camion (m) | lorry |
| car (m) | coach |
| ferry (m) | ferry |
| métro (m) | underground train, metro, tube |
| mobylette (f) | moped |
| moto (f) | motorbike |
| navire (m) | ship |
| à pied | on foot |
| taxi (m) | taxi |
| TER: train express régional (m) | suburban train |
| TGV: train à grande vitesse (m) | high-speed train |
| train (m) | train |
| tramway (m) | tram |
| transports en commun (m/pl) | public transport |
| vélo (m) | bike |
| voiture (f) | car |
| wagon (m) | carriage (on a train) |
| wagon-lit (m) | sleeper (train) |

## Public transport

| | |
|---|---|
| aéroport (m) | airport |
| arrêt d'autobus (m) | bus stop |
| arrivée (m) | arrival |
| arriver | to arrive |
| atterrir | to land |
| autoroute (m) | motorway |
| billet aller et retour (m) | return ticket |
| billet simple (m) | single ticket |
| billeterie (f) | ticket office |
| carnet (m) | book of metro tickets |
| changer | to change (trains) |
| chauffeur (m) | driver |
| chemin de fer (m) | railway |
| circulation (f) | traffic |

| | |
|---|---|
| composter | to validate a ticket |
| consigne (automatique) (f) | left-luggage office (locker) |
| contrôle des passeports (m) | passport control |
| contrôleur (m) | ticket inspector |
| correspondance (f) | connection (metro) |
| décollage (m) | take-off |
| décoller | to take off (plane) |
| délai (m) | waiting time |
| départ (m) | departure |
| descendre (de) | to get off |
| déviation (f) | diversion / detour |
| direct | direct |
| distributeur de billets (m) | ticket machine |
| embouteillage (m) | traffic jam |
| en (auto)bus | by bus |
| en retard | late / delayed |
| essence (f) | petrol |
| excursion (f) | journey, trip |
| garer la voiture | to park |
| gasoil (m) | diesel |
| gaz d'échappement (m/pl) | exhaust emissions |
| guichet (m) | ticket office |
| horaires (m/pl) | timetable |
| ligne (f) | line / route |
| manquer | to miss |
| monter dans | to get on |
| moteur (m) | engine |
| occupé | occupied, taken (seat) |
| panne (f) | breakdown |
| panneau (m) | sign |
| partir | to depart |
| passager / ère (m/f) | passenger |
| péage (m) | motorway toll |
| piste cyclable (f) | cycle path |
| place (f) | seat on train |
| polluer | to pollute |
| portière (f) | door (of train) |
| priorité (f) | priority |
| prix des billets (m) | fare |
| quai (m) | platform (at station) |
| retard (m) | delay |

| | |
|---|---|
| rouler | to travel, to drive |
| route (f) | road |
| salle d'attente (f) | waiting room |
| sans plomb | unleaded |
| se garer | to park |
| simple (m) | single (ticket) |
| sortie (f) | exit |
| station de métro (f) | underground / tube station |
| station-service (f) | petrol station |
| supplément (m) | supplement |
| tarif (m) | fare |
| ticket (m) | ticket (metro) |
| transports en commun (m/pl) | public transport |
| traversée (f) | crossing (ferry) |
| voie (f) | track (at station) |
| voyage (m) | journey |
| voyageur (m) | traveller |

## Directions

| | |
|---|---|
| excusez-moi | excuse me |
| à droite | on the right |
| à gauche | on the left |
| tout droit | straight on |
| aller | to go |
| carrefour (m) | crossroads |
| carte (f) | map |
| coin (m) | corner |
| continuer | to carry on |
| direction (f) | direction |
| feux (m/pl) | traffic lights |
| loin | far |
| mètre (m) | metre |
| pont (m) | bridge |
| prendre | to take |
| près | near |
| rivière (f) | river |
| rond-point (m) | roundabout |
| rue en sens unique (f) | one-way street |
| situé(e) | situated |
| suivre | to follow |
| traverser | to cross |

**HIGHER H**

| | |
|---|---|
| fleuve (m) | river |
| passage piéton (m) | zebra crossing |
| sens interdit | no entry |

## Now try this

Imagine travelling from your home town to Paris. Try to describe in French all the forms of transport you might need.

# ❹ Customer service and transactions

## Restaurant: drinks

| | |
|---|---|
| bière (f) | beer |
| boisson (f) | drink |
| café (m) | coffee |
| chocolat chaud (m) | hot chocolate |
| cidre (m) | cider |
| eau (f) | water |
| eau minérale (f) | mineral water |
| jus (m) | juice |
| lait (m) | milk |
| limonade (m) | lemonade |
| thé (m) | tea |
| vin (m) | wine |

**H HIGHER**

| | |
|---|---|
| infusion (f) | fruit tea |
| lait entier (m) | full-fat milk |

## Restaurant: food

| | |
|---|---|
| abricot (m) | apricot |
| agneau (m) | lamb |
| ananas (m) | pineapple |
| banane (f) | banana |
| beurre (m) | butter |
| bifteck (m) | steak |
| bœuf (m) | beef |
| boulettes (f/pl) | meatballs |
| brochette (f) | kebab |
| cèpe (m) | mushroom |
| céréales (f/pl) | cereal |
| cerise (f) | cherry |
| chips (m/pl) | crisps |
| chocolat (m) | chocolate |
| chou (m) | cabbage |
| chou de bruxelles (m) | Brussels sprout |
| chou-fleur (m) | cauliflower |
| citron (m) | lemon |
| concombre (m) | cucumber |
| confiture (f) | jam |
| côtelette (f) | chop (e.g. pork) |
| des spaghettis | spaghetti |
| escargots (m/pl) | snails |
| fraise (f) | strawberry |
| framboise (f) | raspberry |
| frites (f/pl) | chips |

| | |
|---|---|
| fromage (m) | cheese |
| haricots verts (m/pl) | green beans |
| huile (f) | oil |
| jambon (m) | ham |
| légume (m) | vegetable |
| moutarde (f) | mustard |
| œuf (m) | egg |
| pain (m) | bread |
| pamplemousse (f) | grapefruit |
| paquet (m) | packet |
| pâté (m) | pâté |
| pâtes (f/pl) | pasta |
| pâtisseries (f/pl) | pastries, cakes |
| pêche (f) | peach |
| petit pain (m) | bread roll |
| poire (f) | pear |
| poisson (m) | fish |
| poivre (m) | pepper |
| pomme (f) | apple |
| porc (m) | pork |
| poulet (m) | chicken |
| prune (f) | plum |
| radis (m) | radish |
| raisins (m/pl) | grapes |
| riz (m) | rice |
| salade verte (f) | lettuce |
| salé(e) | salty / savoury |
| sandwich (m) | sandwich |
| sauce (f) | gravy, sauce |
| saucisse (f) | sausage |
| saucisson (m) | cold sliced meat |
| sel (m) | salt |
| soupe (f) | soup |
| steak hâché (m) | mince |
| sucre (m) | sugar |
| tarte aux pommes (f) | apple tart |
| thon(m) | tuna |
| vanille (f) | vanilla |
| viande (f) | meat |
| vinaigre (m) | vinegar |
| yaourt (m) | yoghurt |

carotte (f)

champignon (m)

oignon (m)

petit pois (m/pl)

poivron (m)

pomme de terre (f)

tomate (f)

**H HIGHER**

| | |
|---|---|
| ail (m) | garlic |
| artichaut (m) | artichoke |
| canard (m) | duck |
| crudités (f/pl) | raw vegetables |
| dinde (f) | turkey |
| entrecôte (f) | steak |
| épinards (m/pl) | spinach |
| fromage de chèvre (m) | goat's cheese |
| fruits de mer (m/pl) | seafood |
| laitue (f) | lettuce |
| miel (f) | honey |
| nouilles (f/pl) | noodles |
| poireaux (m/pl) | leeks |
| saumon (m) | salmon |
| truite (f) | trout |

## Now try this

To help you learn the food words, write out the French words in two lists: foods that are healthy and foods that are unhealthy. Then memorise five foods that you like and five foods that you dislike.

# ❹ Customer service and transactions

## Cafés and restaurants

| | |
|---|---|
| addition (f) | bill |
| assiette (f) | plate |
| Bon appétit! | Enjoy your meal! |
| bouteille (f) | bottle |
| carte (f) | menu |
| carte de crédit (f) | credit card |
| choix (m) | choice |
| client(e) (m/f) | customer |
| commander | to order |
| couteau (m) | knife |
| couvert (m) | cutlery (charge at restaurant) |
| cuiller / cuillère (f) | spoon |
| cuit(e) | cooked, boiled |
| déjeuner (m) | lunch |
| délicieux/euse | delicious |
| demander | to ask |
| dessert (m) | dessert |
| dîner (m) | evening meal, dinner, supper |
| entrée (f) | starter, first course |
| fermé (le lundi) | closed (on Mondays) |
| fourchette (f) | fork |
| glacier (m) | ice cream parlour |
| hors d'œuvre (m) | starter |
| journée de repos (f) | day off |
| mélangé(e) | mixed |
| menu à la carte | menu |
| menu du jour (m) | menu of the day |
| menu fixe (m) | fixed price menu, set meal |
| Monsieur! / Garçon! | Waiter! |
| nappe (f) | table cloth |
| petit déjeuner (m) | breakfast |
| petite cuiller / cuillère (f) | teaspoon |
| plat du jour (m) | dish of the day |
| plat principal (m) | main course |
| rôti | roast |
| savoureux/euse | tasty |

| | |
|---|---|
| serveur/euse (m/f) | waiter / waitress |
| spécialité (f) | speciality |
| sucré(e) | sweet |
| végétarien(ne) | vegetarian |
| verre (m) | glass |

**HIGHER H**

| | |
|---|---|
| à point | medium (steak) |
| amer / amère | bitter |
| bien cuit(e) | well-cooked |
| casse-croûte (m) | snack |
| cru(e) | raw |
| épicé(e) | spicy |
| fait maison | home-made |
| fumé(e) | smoked |
| saignant | rare (steak) |

## Shopping: general

| | |
|---|---|
| à la mode | fashionable |
| à un prix bas | low-priced |
| achats (m/pl) | purchases |
| acheter | to buy |
| cabine d'essayage (f) | changing room |
| caisse (f) | till, check-out |
| centre commercial (m) | shopping centre |
| chariot (m) | shopping trolley |
| cher / chère | expensive |
| billet de 10€ (m) | a €10 note |
| client(e) (m/f) | customer |
| commerçant(e) (m/f) | shopkeeper |
| commerce (m) | shop |
| de taille moyenne | medium (size) |
| démodé(e) | old-fashioned |
| dépenser | to spend |
| emballer | to pack / wrap |
| essayer | to try on |
| faire des courses / du shopping | to shop, go shopping |
| faire la queue | to queue |
| heures d'ouverture (f/pl) | opening hours |
| liste de courses (f) | shopping list |

| | |
|---|---|
| livre (f) | pound (in weight) |
| marque (f) | make, brand |
| monnaie (f) | change (coins) |
| offre spéciale (f) | special offer |
| pas cher / chère | cheap |
| pièce (f) | coin |
| pièce de 2€ (f) | a €2 coin |
| prix (m) | price |
| qualité (f) | quality |
| quantité (f) | quantity |
| rayé(e) | striped |
| rayon (m) | department |
| reçu (m) | receipt |
| réduction (f) | discount |
| réduit(e) | reduced |
| sac à main (m) | handbag |
| sac à provisions (m) | shopping bag |
| soldes (m/pl) | sale |
| sortie (de secours) (f) | (emergency) exit |
| taille (f) | size |

**HIGHER H**

| | |
|---|---|
| date limite de consommation (f) | best-before date |
| de bon marché | cheap, value for money |
| emballage (m) | packaging |
| étiquette (f) | label |
| faire un paquet-cadeau | to gift-wrap |
| liquidation du stock (f) | clearance sale |
| serré(e) | tight |
| soldé(e) | reduced |
| soldes (m/pl) | (clearance) sale |

**Now try this**

Cover up the English vocabulary above and make a note of any French words you don't recognise.
Learn these words, then try again in a week's time and see how many words you still don't recognise.

# ❹ Customer service and transactions

## Shops

| | |
|---|---|
| bijouterie (f) | jewellers |
| boucherie (f) | butcher's |
| boucherie-chevaline (f) | horsemeat butcher's |
| boulangerie (f) | baker's |
| charcuterie (f) | delicatessen |
| confiserie (f) | sweet shop |
| épicerie (f) | grocer's, corner shop |
| grand magasin (m) | department store |
| librairie (f) | bookshop |
| magasin (m) | shop |
| marchand de légumes (m) | greengrocer's |
| marché (m) | market |
| papeterie (f) | stationer's |
| parfumerie (f) | perfumery |
| pâtisserie (f) | cake shop |
| pharmacie (f) | chemist's |
| poissonnerie (f) | fishmonger's |

chaussette (f)

ceinture (f)

écharpe (f)

chaussure (f)

chapeau (m)

cravate (f)

## Shopping: clothes

| | |
|---|---|
| baskets (f/pl) | trainers |
| botte (f) | boot |
| boucle d'oreille (f) | earring |
| bracelet (m) | bracelet |
| caleçon (m) | boxers, leggings |
| casquette (f) | cap |
| chemise (f) | shirt |
| chemise de nuit (f) | nightdress, nightie |
| chemisier (m) | blouse |
| collant (m) | tights |
| collier (m) | necklace |
| complet (m) | suit |
| coton (m) | cotton |
| cuir (m) | leather |
| culotte (f) | pants, briefs |
| gant (m) | glove |
| imperm(éable) (m) | raincoat |
| jean (m) | jeans |
| jupe (f) | skirt |
| laine (f) | wool |
| maillot de bain (m) | swimming costume / trunks |
| manteau (m) | coat |
| montre (f) | watch |
| pantalon (m) | trousers |
| pantoufle (f) | slipper |

| | |
|---|---|
| polo (m) | polo shirt |
| pull, pullover (m) | jumper, sweater |
| pyjama (m) | pyjamas |
| short (m) | shorts |
| slip (m) | underpants |
| soie | silk |
| soutien-gorge (m) | bra |
| survêtement (m) | tracksuit |
| sweat (m) | sweatshirt |
| veste (f) | jacket |
| vêtements (m/pl) | clothes |

## Dealing with problems

| | |
|---|---|
| accueil (m) | customer service |
| argent (m) | money |
| bureau des objets trouvés (m) | lost property office |
| carte bancaire (f) | bank card |
| carte d'identité (f) | identity card |
| carte de crédit (m) | credit card |
| cassé(e) | broken |
| changer (de l'argent) | to change (money) |
| chèque (de voyage) (m) | (traveller's) cheque |
| commissariat (m) | police station |
| compte bancaire (m) | bank account |
| cours d'échange (m) | exchange rate |
| dégâts (m/pl) | damage |
| dommage (m) | pity, shame |
| erreur (f) | mistake |
| être remboursé(e) | to get one's money back |
| formulaire (m) | form |
| garder | to keep |

| | |
|---|---|
| gendarme (m) | policeman |
| gendarmerie (f) | police station |
| hôpital (m) | hospital |
| oublier | to forget, leave behind |
| panne (f) | breakdown |
| patron(ne) (f) | boss |
| perdre | to lose |
| policier / femme policier (m/f) | policeman/ woman |
| portefeuille (m) | wallet |
| porte-monnaie (m) | purse |
| problème (m) | problem |
| reçu (m) | receipt |
| se plaindre | to complain |
| service (m) | service |
| vérité (f) | truth |
| vol (m) | theft |
| voleur/euse (m/f) | thief |

**HIGHER H**

| | |
|---|---|
| assurance (f) | insurance |
| assurer | to insure |
| déchiré(e) | torn |
| disparaître | to disappear |
| endommager | to damage |
| prouver | to prove |
| résoudre | to deal with, solve |
| tâche (f) | stain |
| trou (m) | hole |

## Now try this

Look at the clothes that you and your friends are wearing today. Check that you can translate them all into French.

# ❺ Future plans, education and work

## School subjects

| | |
|---|---|
| allemand (m) | German |
| art dramatique (m) | drama |
| arts ménagers (m/pl) | cookery, food technology |
| biologie (f) | biology |
| commerce (m) | business studies |
| économie (f) | economics |
| EPS: éducation physique et sportive (f) | PE |
| EMT: éducation manuelle et technique (f) | technology |
| espagnol (m) | Spanish |
| étude des médias | media studies |
| français (m) | French |
| géographie (f) | geography |
| histoire-géo (f) | history and geography |
| informatique (f) | ICT |
| instruction civique (f) | PSCHE |
| italien (f) | Italian |
| langues étrangères (f/pl) | foreign languages |
| langues vivantes (f/pl) | modern languages |
| matière (f) | subject |
| physique (f) | physics |
| religion (f) | religion, RE |
| sciences (f/pl) | sciences |
| sciences naturelles (f/pl) | biology |
| sciences physiques (f/pl) | physics and chemistry |
| sociologie (f) | sociology |
| technologie (f) | technology, D&T |

## Uniform

| | |
|---|---|
| chaussette (f) | sock |
| chaussure (f) | shoe |
| chemise (f) | shirt |
| cravate (f) | tie |
| jupe (f) | skirt |
| pantalon (m) | trousers |
| pull(over) (m) | pullover |
| sweat (m) | sweatshirt |
| uniforme (m) | uniform |
| veste (f) | blazer / jacket |

## School years

| | |
|---|---|
| année scolaire (f) | school year |
| en cinquième (f) | in year 8 |
| en première (f) | in year 12 |
| en quatrième (f) | in year 9 |
| en seconde (f) | in year 11 |
| en sixième (f) | in year 7 |
| en terminale (f) | in year 13 |
| en troisième (f) | in year 10 |

## School facilities

| | |
|---|---|
| bibliothèque (f) | library |
| bureau de l'école | school office |
| cantine (f) | canteen |
| couloir (m) | corridor |
| cour de récréation (f) | playground |
| gymnase (m) | gym |
| hall de l'école (m) | school hall |
| laboratoire (f) | laboratory |
| salle de classe (f) | classroom |
| salle de sport (f) | sports hall, gym |
| salle des profs (f) | staff room |
| terrain de sport (m) | sports field |
| vestiaires (m/pl) | changing room |

Mathématiques ● maths

Anglais ● English

Histoire ● history

Dessin ● art

Chimie ● chemistry

Musique ● music

## Now try this

What GCSEs are you and your friends taking? Check that you can translate them all into French. If you're thinking of doing A levels, can you translate those too?

# ❺ Future plans, education and work

## School: general

| | |
|---|---|
| apprendre | to learn |
| apprentissage (m) | apprenticeship |
| bac(calauréat) (m) | equivalent of GCE A levels |
| brevet (m) | GCSE equivalent |
| bulletin scolaire (m) | report |
| cahier (m) | exercise book |
| calculatrice (f) | calculator |
| car de ramassage (m) | school bus |
| cartable (m) | school bag |
| certificat de fin des études (m) | school leaving certificate |
| CES: collège d'enseignement secondaire (m) | secondary school |
| concierge (m/f) | caretaker |
| conseiller/ère d'orientation (m/f) | careers adviser |
| contrôle (m) | test, assessment |
| copier | to copy |
| corriger | to correct |
| devoirs (m/pl) | homework |
| dictionnaire (m) | dictionary |
| diplôme (m) | qualification |
| échouer à | to fail (an exam) |
| école primaire (f) | primary school |
| élève (m/f) | pupil |
| emploi du temps (m) | timetable |
| enseigner | to teach |
| équipe (f) | team |
| étudiant(e) (m/f) | student |
| étudier | to study |
| examen (m) | examination |
| excursion scolaire (f) | school trip |
| exercice (m) | task, exercise |
| expérience (f) | experiment |
| facile | easy |
| faible | weak, bad at (subject) |
| faire attention | to pay attention, to watch out, to be careful |

| | |
|---|---|
| feutre (m) | felt tip pen |
| fiche de travail (f) | work sheet |
| formation (f) | training |
| fort(e) | strong, good at (subject) |
| grandes vacances (f/pl) | summer holidays |
| journée scolaire (f) | school day |
| livre d'école (m) | school book |
| lycée (m) | sixth form college |
| LEP: lycée d'enseignement professionel (m) | vocational school |
| maternelle (f) | nursery school |
| niveau (m) | achievement, level |
| note (f) | mark, grade |
| passer un examen | to take / sit an exam |
| principal (m) | headteacher |
| prof (m/f) | teacher |
| professeur (m) | teacher |
| progrès (m) | progress |
| récréation, récré (f) | break |
| redoubler | to repeat a year |
| règle (f) | rule |
| rentrée (f) | first day back |
| repas (m) | meal |
| résultat (m) | result |
| retenue (f) | detention |
| réussir à | to pass (exam) |
| réussite (f) | success |
| réviser | to revise |
| semestre (m) | semester |
| sérieux/euse | serious (hardworking) |
| sévère | strict |
| stylo (m) | (ballpoint) pen |
| tableau (m) | whiteboard / blackboard |
| travailler dur | to work hard |
| travailleur/euse | hardworking |
| trimestre (m) | term |
| vacances (f/pl) | holidays |

| | |
|---|---|
| annuler | to cancel |
| autorisation (f) | permission |
| bachelier/ière (m/f) | student who has passed the bac |
| bic (m) | ballpoint pen |
| cahier d'appel (m) | register |
| cartouche (d'encre) (f) | ink cartridge |
| doué(e) | gifted |
| écrire des lignes | written punishment, lines |
| enseigner | to teach |
| épeler | to spell |
| être en retenue | to have a detention |
| études (f/pl) | studies |
| examen final (m) | final exam |
| expliquer | to explain |
| facultatif/ive | optional (subject) |
| internat (m) | boarding school |
| laisser tomber | to drop a subject |
| licence (f) | degree (university) |
| manuel (m) | textbook |
| nécessaire | necessary |
| obligatoire | core / compulsory |
| passer (en classe supérieure) | to move up (to next year) |
| pensionnat (m) | boarding school |
| perfectionner | to improve |
| perte de temps (f) | waste of time |
| poser une question | to ask a question |
| rédaction (f) | essay |
| sécher les cours | to skive / skip lessons |

## Now try this

Pick out all of the stationery items on the page and make learning cards for them. Write the French word on one side and a picture or the English meaning on the other side. Then test yourself on them.

# ❺ Future plans, education and work

## Job adverts

| | |
|---|---|
| acteur / actrice (m/f) | actor |
| agent de police (m) | police officer |
| annonce (f) | advert (job) |
| architecte (m) | architect |
| candidature (f) | application |
| compagnie (f) | company |
| cuisinier/ière (m/f) | cook |
| de l'heure | per hour |
| dentiste (m) | dentist |
| électricien(ne) | electrician |
| emploi (m) | job |
| entretien (m) | interview |
| fermier/ière (m/f) | farmer |
| fonctionnaire (m/f) | civil servant |
| formation (f) | training |
| heures de travail (f/pl) | hours of work |
| hôtesse / steward de l'air (m/f) | air hostess / steward |
| infirmier/ière (m/f) | nurse |
| informaticien(ne) (m/f) | computer scientist |
| ingénieur (m) | engineer |
| journaliste (m/f) | journalist |
| maçon (m) | builder |
| mécanicien(ne) (m/f) | mechanic |
| médecin (m) | doctor |
| offres d'emploi (f/pl) | situations vacant |
| plombier (m) | plumber |
| pompier (m) | firefighter |
| poser sa candidature | to apply for a job |
| possibilités d'avancement (f/pl) | promotion prospects |
| programmeur/euse | programmer |
| remplir un formulaire | to fill in a form |
| stage (en entreprise) (m) | work experience |
| technicien(ne) | technician |
| travail (m) | work |

## Job applications

| | |
|---|---|
| l'année prochaine (f) | next year |
| annonce (f) | advert |
| apprenti(e) (m/f) | apprentice |
| apprentissage (m) | apprenticeship |
| boulot (m) | work |
| bulletin scolaire (m) | school report |
| candidature (f) | application |
| certificat de fin des études secondaires | school leaving certificate |
| ci-inclus | enclosed |
| CV (m) | CV |
| diplômé(e) | qualified |
| diplôme (m) | qualification |
| éducation | school education |
| entretien (m) | interview |
| envoyer | to send |
| expérience du travail (f) | experience of work |
| expérimenté(e) | experienced |
| formation (f) | training |
| formulaire (m) | form |
| impression (f) | impression |
| joindre | to enclose, to attach |
| lettre (f) | letter |
| lettre de candidature (f) | letter of application |
| métier (m) | profession, job, occupation |
| offre d'emploi (f) | job advert |
| poser sa candidature | to apply for a job |
| qualifié(e) | qualified |
| rendez-vous (m) | appointment |
| réussi(e) | successful |
| réussite (f) | success |
| se présenter | to introduce oneself |
| stage en entreprise (m) | work experience |
| succès (m) | success |
| travail (m) | job, work |
| université (f) | university |

## Internet language

| | |
|---|---|
| CD-rom (m) | CD ROM |
| charger | to load |
| chatter | to chat (online) |
| clavier (m) | keyboard |
| copier | to burn |
| courrier électronique (m) | e-mail |
| écran (m) | screen |
| effacer | to erase, delete |
| e-mail (m) | e-mail |
| forum (m) | chatroom |
| imprimante (f) | printer |
| imprimer | to print |
| internet (m) | internet |
| lien (m) | connection, link |
| logiciel (m) | software |
| mettre en ligne | to upload |
| mot de passe (m) | password |
| numérique | digital |
| ordinateur (m) | computer |
| page internet (m) | internet page |
| page web (f) | webpage |
| page d'accueil (f) | homepage |
| programmeur (m) | programmer |
| sauvegarder | to save, to store |
| site internet / web (m) | website |
| slash (m) | forward slash |
| sondage (m) | opinion poll / survey |
| souris (f) | mouse |
| taper | to type |
| télécharger | to download |
| toile (f) | web |
| touche (f) | key (of keyboard) |
| virus (m) | virus |
| web (m) | web |
| webcam (f) | webcam |

**HIGHER**

| | |
|---|---|
| à / arobase | at: @ in email address |
| base de données (f) | database |
| disque dur (m) | hard disk |
| écran tactile (m) | touch screen |
| fichier (m) | (data) file |
| soulignement (m) | underscore |
| traitement de texte (m) | word processing |

## Now try this

To help you learn the jobs vocabulary, make a list of five jobs that you would like to do and five that you would not like to do. Then memorise them.

# Answers

## Personal information

### Birthdays

1 Name: Benoît
Age: 16
Birthday: 21 December
2 Name: Jean-Marc
Age: 17
Birthday: 30 March
3 Name: Véronique
Age: 19
Birthday: 1 July
4 Name: Alizée
Age: 13
Birthday: 23 June

### Character description

B, D, E, G

### Describing my family

1 Because he is now married.
2 She is always asking questions.
3 For her judo lessons.
4 When she has difficulties with it.

### Sport

(a) Past
(b) Present
(c) Future
(d) Future

### Going out

(a) the swimming pool
(b) do homework
(c) the leisure centre
(d) walk the dog

### Weekends

1 It was fine and warm.
2 Have a picnic and swim in the lake.
3 She had an accident (a car came too quickly out of a small street).
4 She spent the weekend in bed, and has her leg in plaster so has to walk with crutches.

### Cinema

A, D, E

### Online activities

1 A    2 E    3 B    4 C

### Daily routine

1 C    2 A    3 B    4 C

### Healthy eating

(a) Rémi
(b) Jean
(c) Gisèle

### Health problems

(a) Freya
(b) Freya
(c) Grandad
(d) Alain

## Out and about

### Things to do in town

(a) C
(b) E
(c) B
(d) F

### Signs around town

1 bakery
2 in advance
3 Sunday

### Travelling by train

1 (a) 19h58
  (b) 21h24
  (c) you have to change at Marseille
3 (a) 16h53
  (b) 19h01
  (c) customer just wants a single ticket
4 (a) 18h10
  (b) 22h42
  (c) there is an hour's delay

### Weather

A, C, F, H

### Describing a town

1 B    2 C    3 C

### Holiday destinations

(a) Célia
(b) Murielle
(c) Rayan
(d) Murielle
(e) Célia

### Staying in a hotel

1 to the Midi (south of France)
2 for young people: swimming pool / games room; for older people: air conditioning / a lift
3 Any two of: they couldn't see the beach (from their room) / it was too noisy to sleep at night / the hotel was still being built / the air conditioning didn't work / there was nothing for the children to do.
4 they will never go to that hotel again

### Holiday activities

C, E, F, G

### Booking accommodation

1 C    2 C

### Holiday experiences

1 his best friend, Brice
2 it was for 13–17 year-olds
3 in an enormous chalet; they shared a room with two other boys
4 because they were really hungry

### Directions

A Pour aller (à la gare), vous tournez à gauche, puis tournez à droite. Allez tout droit aux feux et la gare est située sur votre (droite / gauche).
C Pour aller (à la gare) vous prenez la deuxième rue à droite, tournez à droite aux feux, et la gare est située sur votre gauche.

### Public transport

(a) the Channel
(b) a little
(c) bikes
(d) on the bus

### Transport

(a) Germany
(b) A9
(c) at 21.30
(d) a broken-down lorry

## Customer service and transactions

### At the café
1 E    2 C    3 F    4 D

### Eating in a café
Olivier: B
Adèle: B

### Eating in a restaurant
(a) Malik
(b) Léna
(c) Laetitia
(d) Malik

### Restaurant review
(a) cold
(b) wine
(c) something was lost

### Shops
1 (e)    2 (c)    3 (d)
4 (b)    5 (a)

### Shopping for food
(a) 10
(b) 1 kilo (a packet)
(c) 12
(d) 1 jar
(e) 12
(f) 3 bottles

### Shopping
1 link your MP3 player to the receiver in the hat
2 in your pocket or bag
3 not more than 12 metres away
4 none

### Signs in shops
C

### Clothes and colours
1 B    2 C    3 A    4 D

### Internet shopping
1 B    2 C    3 F

### Money
1 A    2 E    3 D

## Future plans, education and work

### School life
(b) Hubert
(c) Justine
(d) Roxanne
(e) Hubert

### Primary school
C

### Issues at school
(ii) C    (iii) F
(iv) D    (v) E

### In the future
Lola: C    Éva: F
Maël: A    Yanis: E

### Jobs
1 works long hours
2 computer scientist
3 in an office (in front of a computer)
4 very boring
5 hairdresser
6 two days a week

### Job adverts
(a) keen
(b) outdoors
(c) seven
(d) most suitable

### Job application
(a) ii    (b) ii

### Job interview
(a) 18
(b) yes
(c) has two brothers and gets on well with them; they play football and she babysits them
(d) calm / kind / strict if necessary
(e) by text

### Opinions about jobs
(a) Zoë    (b) Léna
(c) Noah    (d) Léna
(e) Zoë    (f) Noah

### Work experience
B, D, E, H

### Computers
*Two of:* it is simple / efficient / free

## Grammar

### Articles 1
le garçon    la mère
les étudiants    le printemps
l'Espagne    la Loire
la condition    le bleu
la décision    le père
le garage    la plage

### Articles 2
1 (a) Allez au
   (b) Allez aux
   (c) Allez à la
   (d) Allez à l'
   (e) Allez aux
   (f) Allez au
   (g) Allez au
   (h) Allez à la

2 (a) Je veux du pain.
   (b) Avez-vous du lait?
   (c) Il n'a pas d'essence.
   (d) Je vais á l'école.
   (e) Est-ce que tu vas à la mairie?
   (f) Il va aux toilettes.

### Adjectives
1 un petit chien noir
2 la semaine dernière
3 Mon petit frère est très actif.
4 Ma meilleure amie est petite et timide.
5 Son frère est grand, sportif mais un peu sérieux.

### Possessives
mon frère    ses amis
son ami    son portable
ses amis    mes parents
son sac    leur ami
ma sœur    leurs amis
son amie    leur voiture

### Comparing things
1 L'Everest est la montagne **la plus haute** du monde.
2 La veste est **plus chère** que la robe.
3 Demain il fera **plus beau** qu'aujourd'hui.
4 **La meilleure** solution est de prendre le train.
5 Julie est **moins intelligente** que Fabien.
6 Le TGV est le train **le plus rapide.**

## Other adjectives

1 Noé veut cette veste.
Laquelle?
Celle-ci.

2 Je préfère ce portable.
Lequel?
Celui-ci.

3 Manon a choisi ces chaussures.
Lesquelles?
Celles-ci.

4 Son frère achète ces jeux.
Lesquels?
Ceux-là.

5 On regarde ce film ce soir.
Lequel?
Celui-là

## Adverbs

*(possible answer)*

Notre chat a disparu. **D'habitude**, il rentre chaque soir, **toujours** vers six heures. **Soudain**, j'ai entendu un bruit. **Très doucement** j'ai ouvert la porte et j'ai été **vraiment** surpris de voir Max avec trois petit chatons! **Finalement,** Il est entré dans la maison. **Évidemment**, Max n'est plus Max, mais Maxine!

## Object pronouns

1 Il l'a envoyé.
2 Je ne l'ai pas regardée.
3 Il ne les a pas achetées.
4 Tu l'as vu?
5 Sarah l'a lu.
6 Mes parents l'ont achetée.

## More pronouns: *y* and *en*

1 J'**y** suis déjà allé.
2 J'**en** ai déjà mangé trop.
3 J'**y** suis allé hier.
4 J'**y** vais de temps en temps.
5 On **y** va souvent.
6 Je n'**en** mange jamais.

## Other pronouns

1 Mon ami **qui** s'appelle Bruno est fana de football.
2 L'émission **que** j'ai vue hier n'était pas passionnante.
3 Le quartier **où** ils habitent est vraiment calme.
4 Le prof **dont** je vous ai déjà parlé.
5 Elle a une sœur **qui** est prof.
6 J'ai accepté le stage **que** mon prof m'a proposé.

## Present tense: -ER verbs

Je **m'appelle** Lou. J'ai une sœur qui **s'appelle** Marina et qui **joue** au tennis. Je **préfère** faire de la danse. Je **chante** et je **joue** de la guitare. Le soir nous **rentrons** à cinq heures et nous **mangeons** un casse-croûte. Puis je **tchate** avec mes amis, et j'**écoute** de la musique. Quelquefois mon frère et moi **jouons** aux jeux vidéo ou **téléchargeons** un film pour regarder plus tard.

## -IR and -RE verbs

1 Le matin je **sors** à sept heures et demie.
2 Le mardi les cours **finissent** à cinq heures.
3 Mon copain et moi ne **buvons** pas de coca.
4 Le train **part** à 8h20.
5 Nous **apprenons** l'espagnol.
6 Pendant les vacances nous **dormons** sous la tente.
7 Mes copains **choisissent** des frites.

## *avoir* and *être*

1 Nous **avons** un petit chaton. Il est tout noir mais il **a** les yeux verts. Il **a** toujours faim. Il **a** beaucoup de jouets mais j'**ai** une balle de ping pong qu'il adore et mon petit frère **a** un petit oiseau en fourrure qu'il déchire. **As**-tu un animal?

2 Je **suis** britannique. Je suis né en Angleterre. Mes parents **sont** italiens. Ils **sont** nés en Italie mais ils habitent ici depuis vingt ans. Mon frère **est** sportif. Il **est** champion régional de judo. Ma sœur **est** paresseuse. En revanche je **suis** charmant!

## *aller* and *faire*

1 (a) Je **vais** au collège à huit heures.
   (b) Nous y **allons** en car de ramassage.
   (c) Le soir on **va** au centre de sports.
   (d) Ma sœur **va** à la piscine et moi, je **vais** au gymnase.
   (e) Mes parents **vont** au bar, avec les autres parents!

(a) I go to school at 8 o'clock.
(b) We go in the school bus.
(c) In the evening we go to the sports centre.
(d) My sister goes to the swimming pool and I go to the gymnasium.
(e) My parents go to the bar with the other parents!

2 En hiver je **fais** du ski. Mon frère **fait** du surf et mes parents **font** aussi du ski. Ma sœur ne **fait** pas de ski mais nous **faisons** du patinage ensemble. Que **faites**-vous?
In winter I go skiing. My brother goes surfing and my parents also go skiing. My sister doesn't ski but we go skating together. What do you do?

## Modal verbs

1 (a) Martin veut y aller mais il ne peut pas.
   (b) Nous voulons y aller mais nous ne pouvons pas.
   (c) Vous voulez y aller mais vous ne pouvez pas.
   (d) Mes parents veulent y aller mais ils ne peuvent pas.

2 (a) Je dois faire mes devoirs.
   (b) Je ne sais pas faire les maths.
   (c) Sais-tu faire le français?
   (d) On doit apprendre les verbes.
   (e) Mes copains français doivent écrire une dissertation.
   (f) Je ne dois pas écrire de dissertation – je ne dois que répondre aux questions.

### Reflexive verbs

Je ne **m'entends** pas bien avec mon grand frère. Il **se moque** de moi. Nous **nous disputons** souvent. Je **m'entends** mieux avec ma sœur. On **s'amuse** bien ensemble. Nous **nous couchons** de bonne heure parce que le matin nous **nous levons** à six heures – nous, c'est-à-dire toute la famille sauf mon frère qui ne **se réveille** pas. Quand finalement il **se lève** il ne **se douche** pas parce qu'il n'a pas le temps.

### The perfect tense 1

Mercredi dernier **j'ai pris** le bus pour aller en ville. J'y **ai rencontré** un ami. Nous **avons fait** les magasins. J'**ai voulu** acheter des baskets rouges mais elles étaient trop chères. Nous **avons mangé** des burgers et comme boisson j'**ai choisi** un coca. Mon copain **a bu** un milkshake fraise. J'**ai laissé** mon sac au bar. Je devais y retourner mais par conséquent j'**ai raté** le bus et j'**ai dû** rentrer à pied.

### The perfect tense 2

1 Samedi dernier je **me suis levé(e)** de bonne heure.
2 Le matin je **suis allé(e)** jouer au football.
3 Je **suis sorti(e)** à dix heures.
4 L'autre équipe **n'est pas venue**.
5 Nous y **sommes restés** une heure, puis nous **sommes rentrés**.
6 Je **suis arrivé(e)** à la maison juste avant midi.

### The imperfect tense

It's written in the imperfect because it's about what someone used to do.

Quand j'**étais** jeune, j'**habitais** à la campagne. Nous **avions** un grand jardin où je **jouais** au foot avec mes frères. Le samedi on **allait** au marché en ville. Il y **avait** beaucoup de vendeurs de fruits et légumes et un kiosque à journaux où j'**achetais** des bonbons. Nous **mangions** des merguez (des saucisses épicées) et nous **buvions** du coca. On **rentrait** en bus avec tous nos voisins et nos achats!

### The future tense

L'année prochaine nous **irons** en France. Nous **prendrons** l'Eurostar. On **partira** de Londres et on **arrivera** à Paris. Puis on **changera** de train et on **continuera** vers le sud. Nous **ferons** du camping. Mes parents **dormiront** dans une caravane mais je **dormirai** sous une tente. Pendant la journée nous **irons** sur la plage et **jouerons** au basket et au tennis. Le soir on **mangera** au resto. On **se fera** des amis.

### The conditional

1 Je **voudrais** aller en Italie.
2 Si j'avais assez d'argent, j'**irais** en Inde.
3 Nous **pourrions** faire un long voyage.
4 Tu **aimerais** voir ce film?
5 Je **préférerais** manger au restaurant.
6 Si j'avais faim, je **mangerais** une pizza.
7 Il **voudrait** aller en ville samedi.
8 On **pourrait** aller à la patinoire cet après-midi?
9 Tu **verrais** le match si tu restais encore deux jours.
10 Vous **voudriez** quelque chose à boire?

### The pluperfect tense

pluperfect verbs: 1–6

imperfect verb: 7, 11

perfect verbs: 8, 9, 10

### Negatives

1h, 2f, 3b, 4a, 5c, 6e, 7d, 8g

(a) Tu ne fais rien.
(b) Tu ne m'as jamais aidé à la maison.
(c) Tu ne fais plus tes devoirs.
(d) Tu ne respectes personne.
(e) Tu ne fais que le nécessaire.
(f) Tu ne peux aller ni au football ni au restaurant ce soir.

### Questions

Où travaille ton père? Where does your father work?

Qui va à la fête? Who is going to the party?

Comment allez-vous? How are you?

Combien d'amis as-tu sur Facebook? How many friends do you have on Facebook?

À quelle heure rentrent tes parents? What time are your parents coming home?

Pourquoi as-tu raté le bus? Why did you miss the bus?

Que voulez-vous faire? What do you want to do?

Depuis quand apprends-tu le français? How long have you been learning French?

### Useful little words
*(possible answers)*

1 partout
2 sous
3 dans
4 derrière
5 puis
6 dehors
7 dans
8 sans
9 à la fin
10 dans
11 au
12 sous